# LOST
## BLUEGRASS

*History of a Vanishing Landscape*

D1414004

RONNIE DREISTADT

Charleston · London

THE
History
PRESS

Published by The History Press
Charleston, SC 29403
www.historypress.net

Copyright © 2011 by Ronnie Dreistadt
All rights reserved

Front cover photos courtesy of Alexa Arnold.

First published 2011

Manufactured in the United States

ISBN 978.1.60949.271.7

Library of Congress Cataloging-in-Publication Data

Dreistadt, Ronnie.
Lost Bluegrass : history of a vanishing landscape / Ronnie Dreistadt.
p. cm.
Includes bibliographical references.
ISBN 978-1-60949-271-7
1. Bluegrass Region (Ky.)--History. 2. Bluegrass Region (Ky.)--History, Local. 3. Historic
buildings--Kentucky--Bluegrass Region. 4. Historic sites--Kentucky--Bluegrass Region. 5.
Landscapes--Kentucky--Bluegrass Region--History. 6. Bluegrass Region (Ky.)--Social life
and customs. 7. Bluegrass Region (Ky.)--Biography. I. Title.
F457.B6D74 2011
976.9'3--dc22
201100626

# Contents

# PREFACE

A Hoosier writing a book about the Kentucky Bluegrass? Full disclosure: yes, it's true. Growing up in the knobs of southern Indiana, I couldn't have told you the difference between a Secretariat and a Bombay Duck. That's a big difference—you can look it up. I only vaguely knew a little about the "greatest two minutes in sports" held every first Saturday in May across the river at Churchill Downs, roughly twenty miles from my house. It might as well have been held on the moon.

In 1994, I watched the Louisiana Derby on television to humor a friend who was really into horse racing. I chose a horse to follow named Kandaly (I don't remember why) and watched him run. He left the gate in slow motion and fell so far back that the camera couldn't catch him with the other horses. He lagged probably twenty lengths behind. Then, coming around the far turn, I could see the bright pink silks of his jockey gaining on the others. Kandaly was flying! The deep closer mowed down the competition in the stretch, and Kandaly stamped his ticket to the 1994 Kentucky Derby. Unfortunately, it poured rain for the 1994 Derby, and Kandaly hated the mud, prompting trainer Louis Roussell to scratch him from the race just minutes before the drenched crowd sang, "The sun shines bright on my old Kentucky home."

I was pretty disappointed that "my horse" didn't have a shot at the Derby, but later that year another horse that liked to come flying from way back, Concern, came to Churchill Downs and won the Breeder's Cup Classic. I was there—my first trip ever to a thoroughbred racetrack—and of course I had a little money on the deep closer. In fact, I probably picked every deep closer that day and never won a penny until the Classic. Concern came home, passing Best Pal, Tabasco Cat and Derby winner Go for Gin. I broke even for the day. I was hooked.

I got a job as a part-time tour guide at the Kentucky Derby Museum that next summer, and it was then that I began to really appreciate the history that had taken place under those magnificent Twin Spires for over a century. Names like Citation, Typhoon II, Old Rosebud and Spokane (all winners of the Kentucky Derby) are on plaques lining the grandstand of Churchill Downs, and learning their stories—the people, the farms, the legends behind these horses—fascinated me.

The first Bluegrass thoroughbred farm I ever visited was Claiborne Farm. Always hospitable, the farm staff led out Derby winner Go for Gin, Unbridled, Conquistador Cielo and several others. Pictures were taken, stories were told and questions were answered before we were led back up toward the small parking area. Then, I saw it. In a small courtyard, I saw the tombstone, old and worn from decades of weathering, of 1930 Triple Crown winner Gallant Fox—the Fox of Belair, as he was known in the 1930s. Secretariat's grave was close by. A chill ran down my spine, because it was then that I could feel the aura of the place. These thoroughbreds—living and dead—were not just horses or commodities, and certainly not pets; they were an essential part of the breathing fabric of the historic farm. And not just of this farm, but of the farms up and down Paris Pike, farther past Lexington toward Nicholasville and northward toward the capital, Frankfort. These magnificent horses, now and for many years past, were what much of the region was all about.

After stints at other jobs, but still following the sport, I was hired by the Kentucky Derby Museum to serve as outreach educator. That job entailed traveling the state, going into schools and teaching programs about horses and the Kentucky Derby and tying that information to what the state calls "core content"—or the information teachers are supposed to teach students. The program was, and still is, sponsored by the Kentucky Thoroughbred Association, keeping the programming free for participating schools.

Logging many thousands of miles on Kentucky roadways for the program over the years, this Hoosier has come to love and appreciate the varied sections of Kentucky. It's quite a wide state—431 miles from Hickman, a small town on the Mississippi River bordering Missouri, to South Shore, an even smaller town on the Ohio River bordering Ohio, with diverse regions in between. You'll find ancient Appalachian Mountains with isolated mining communities in the east and hilly knobs in a swath of land swooping down from the Ohio River around Louisville. You'll see some of the most beautiful man-made lakes throughout southern Kentucky and swamps and rolling farmland in western Kentucky. And, of course, in the Bluegrass Region, you'll see many miles of wooden fencing, manicured landscapes and ornate barns, home to the most expensive and well-known thoroughbreds in the world. I have visited many schools in all of these regions, and the pride of being "the home of the Kentucky Derby" and "the horse capital of the world" is evident wherever I visit.

In 2007, the Kentucky Derby Museum, partnered with the University of Kentucky's College of Design, developed a temporary exhibit called Vanishing Bluegrass. Several groups—the Kentucky Heritage Council, the Bluegrass Conservancy and the Bluegrass Trust—assisted in the mounting of the exhibit. The exhibit highlighted the growing concern of suburban sprawl encroaching on previous farmland, as some of these farms were very historic in nature. It was a problem shared by not only concerned Kentuckians but also people all over the world. The inner Bluegrass Region was named one of the World's Most Endangered Sites by the World Monuments Fund in 2006, joining such other renowned American cultural landscapes as the Gulf Coast region, Pennsylvania's Lancaster County and Historic Route 66. The Sierra Club has noted that much of the region is in danger due to unchecked suburban growth.

The region's signature industry—thoroughbreds—has been threatened before. This narrative will briefly discuss two of those threats: the impact of two foraging armies during the Civil War and the impact of the reform movement during the late eighteenth and early nineteenth centuries. The number one problem, and the main topic of our narrative, threatening Kentucky's thoroughbred farms—large, historic, small, locally owned, foreign-owned, thriving or struggling—is suburban sprawl. The farms that I have focused on here were chosen because of the thoroughbred-racing (especially relating to the Kentucky Derby) lens through which I look. Some of the farms chosen may not even be considered victims of traditional sprawl. Some of them may not be victims at all but were developed for the ultimate betterment of the community. That is up to the reader to decide. But that doesn't change the fact that these important places—and I contend that these old farms from the past were and are important places within the Bluegrass Region—are gone and can never be recovered.

The issue of sprawl and land development is controversial, and opinions greatly vary, even within some of the communities and families highlighted. Some may disagree with my conclusions, but this narrative is not meant to be confrontational. Virtually every community struggles with the question: what do we want our town (or countryside) to look like? Not all communities agree on what that should be. It is not my intention to play good guys versus bad guys in this narrative, although I certainly have an idea of what I want the Bluegrass Region to look like. There are many reasons to develop a piece of property, and sometimes it's not just about making a buck. Even when it is, the prospect of financial security for the seller and their families is something many of us would have to think long and hard about if given the opportunity. Also, anyone who farms knows that "land wealthy" doesn't mean "cash wealthy"—driving past a large tract of land, with beautiful thoroughbreds and fancy outbuildings, doesn't necessarily mean that the owner is eating from a silver spoon. Selling a farm for development may not even be about financial security but about financial bailout.

There are important questions to ponder as we learn about farmers past and present in the region: What was their relationship to the farmland they owned? What was their responsibility to their families, to their neighbors and to the community as a whole? All of the farmers and landowners profiled of course had different viewpoints, different goals and different circumstances.

This book will conclude with a look at the individuals and groups who are fighting to protect the thoroughbred industry in the Bluegrass Region. Some groups fight through education and public awareness. Some groups can fight economically through conservation easements. Others fight in the political realm through zoning regulations and environmental law. Few of us can afford to sit this argument out, regardless of where we live.

One other issue that threatens the Bluegrass Region but is not covered within the scope of this narrative are the struggles of Kentucky in competition with other states in the lucrative racing and breeding industries. Other states have supplemented purse structures from expanded gaming—mainly installing slot machines at racetracks, creating "racinos." Currently, neighboring states West Virginia and Indiana allow alternative gaming, luring horsemen to race at their tracks with higher purses, supplemented by the expanded gaming money. This clearly puts Kentucky at a disadvantage and threatens Kentucky's place atop the industry.

It is imperative that we protect the things about Kentucky that make us Kentuckians. Mammoth Cave, bourbon, baseball bats, bluegrass music, college basketball and Corvettes—even the Hatfield-McCoy feud—are all a part of Kentucky culture. But those majestic and powerful horses bred at thoroughbred farms throughout the inner Bluegrass Region, the ones we watch at Churchill Downs every first Saturday in May, are our most famous and one of our most viable economic products. The region has fought off threats before; the devastating effects of the Civil War and the Age of Reform both almost destroyed the thoroughbred industry. But the inner Bluegrass Region is currently locked in a battle with its most formidable foe yet: us.

# I

# A Developing
# Bluegrass Culture

Looking back today, the 1790s in America was an exciting time to be alive. Of course, "in America" meant you were living in one of the original thirteen colonies, and life was probably only exciting if you were fortunate enough to be a part of the gentleman class of the South or a white citizen of the North. It was probably not exciting if you were one of almost 700,000 enslaved people, toiling and in bondage mainly in Virginia and throughout the Tidewater area. In many cases, it was also not that exciting for women, considering their role as caretakers of the family and the fact that many times they were forced to have little contact or knowledge outside of the home.

But philosophical idealisms around the world were shaking things up. Enlightenment ideals, focusing on science and rationalism, challenged long-held beliefs about the foundations of life and human nature itself. The French, inspired by the American version, overthrew its monarchy in the name of republicanism, sparking a long chain of events that eventually resulted in the Napoleonic era at the end of the decade. In the United States, arguments raged about what direction the new nation—or, as Europeans saw it, the "republican experiment"—would go, symbolized by Jefferson's more agrarian-dominated version or Hamilton's urban focus. Another disagreement among citizens was over which example we should most follow for our new nation: Jefferson said France's idealism, while Hamilton maintained English pragmatism. Most people followed these debates

The Inner Bluegrass Region. *Courtesy of the Lexington Visitor and Convention Bureau.*

carefully, but ultimately things were just as they are today—people were trying to make better lives for themselves through work, relationships and, if they were fortunate enough to have any, leisure time.

For many people, that meant leaving home and making their way across the Appalachian Mountains, weaving through the Cumberland Gap and into the western territories for new opportunities. Originally part of Virginia, a series of forts was constructed in the region that would later become

# A Developing Bluegrass Culture

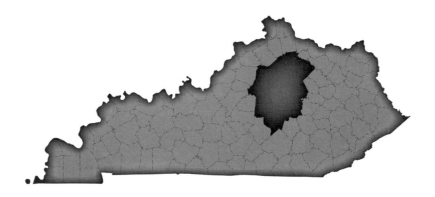

The Inner Bluegrass Region. *Courtesy of the Lexington Visitor and Convention Bureau.*

Kentucky. James Harrod's fort was the earliest permanent settlement in the region. Another early settlement was Fort Logan, completed in 1777, located in what would later be Lincoln County, at the southeastern edge of the Bluegrass Region. These forts served as safe havens against the Native Americans who used Kentucky as a hunting ground and were less than pleased with the settlers' intrusion. The forts were also built because of the tensions with the British, and to a lesser extent the Spanish, in the years preceding the American Revolution. By 1775, four small settlements dotted the Bluegrass Region territory: Harrodsburg, Boonesborough, Boiling Springs and Logan's Station.

What the settlers found once they made it to the region were three distinct geographical areas: the Outer Bluegrass, the Eden Shale Hills and the Inner Bluegrass. The entire region is spread across Ordovician limestone, but differences in the soils created differences in early settlement. The Outer Bluegrass, composed of fertile, reddish soils, produced a concentration of farmers who mainly grew tobacco, corn and hemp. Settlement in most of the Outer Bluegrass, with much of the area located between present-day Cincinnati and Louisville, was rapid because of the transportation and trade advantages of the Ohio River. The Eden Shale Hills, just beyond the deep gorge of the Kentucky River and a transition to the Outer Bluegrass, contains soils that are infertile yellowish clays and steep slopes, making settlement sparse. Settlers were able to farm valley bottoms in this section, but most tended to be small operations. The Inner Bluegrass, composed of deep, fertile soils fed by high levels of phosphorus from the limestone, attracted settlers by the droves, as they found some of the best land for agriculture in the world.

Besides great soil for agriculture, the Inner Bluegrass Region was attractive to pioneers for several other reasons. First, the area was fairly well known due to earlier exploration by Gabriel Woods, John Howard, Christopher Gist and Daniel Boone. Also, there were few dense forests like in other regions, making settlement much less labor-intensive. The region is typically served by a temperate climate, although short pockets of either hot, humid weather in the summer or frigid temperatures in the winter are experienced. Adequate rainfall is also an advantageous aspect of the climate. One settler from Maryland in the late eighteenth century wrote back home, "What would I not give to show you Nature and Nature's works in perfection."[1]

Underground springs feed the lush landscape; the most famous is McConnell Springs, named for a group of settlers who camped at the water source in 1775. Upon learning that a battle had been fought in the American Revolution at Lexington, Massachusetts, the settlement was named Lexington in honor of the battle. Lexington would later be incorporated as a town in 1782, growing to become the urban center for the Inner Bluegrass. These natural springs were often ideal locations for settlements. Close by,

McConnell Springs, where the city of Lexington was founded. *Photo by author.*

Harrodsburg and Georgetown were both founded at locations with large springs as well.

Of course, settlers were not just bringing themselves and their families to the area. Many of them were sons of the large landowners of Virginia and North Carolina and brought the institution of slavery into the region. Farmers who grew labor-intensive crops like tobacco and hemp relied on slave labor to do the work in the fields. They brought livestock with them as well—beef and dairy cattle, poultry and swine and their sturdy workhorses, donkeys and mules. Many of them also brought a distinct cavalier attitude rooted in English traditional society. Karl B. Raitz, in his essay on Bluegrass culture, noted four qualities that this belief system encompassed:

> *Cultural traditions included an aristocratic bent that under-wrote slave holding as a labor force, service in government as a link to prestige and power, large land holdings as a measure of status, and relished gambling, whether it be on horse races or fighting cocks, as an accepted mode of entertainment.*[2]

The horses that most setters brought were here to either work or provide transportation. These animals were sturdy, able to withstand the rigors of pulling a plow or wagon. But the wealthier citizens, the ones described above as embracing the cavalier culture of Virginia, brought with them the "blooded horse," horses bred for characteristics like speed or stamina. The first thoroughbred (although it was not called this yet), a breed developed for racing among the English nobility beginning in the late 1600s, crossed the Atlantic into the New World in 1730. A son of the Byerly Turk, considered one of the three foundation sires for the breed, ended up in the colony of Virginia. His name was Bull Rock. These "thoroughly bred horses" (or, later, thoroughbreds) from one of the three foundation sires were bred to do one thing very well: race with incredible speed over distance.

Other thoroughbreds crossed the Atlantic, and soon, many of them were crossing the Appalachians through the Cumberland Gap, moving into a region that turned out to be a virtual paradise for the breed. The physical confirmation of these thoroughbreds, with a combination of great bursts of acceleration and speed, along with the ability to carry that speed over a distance, made settling in the area, with its lush bluegrass, attractive for the gentleman class. Most thoroughbreds, when fully grown, stand between fifteen and seventeen hands tall from the front hoof to the withers and weigh anywhere from nine hundred to eleven hundred pounds. Very muscular and defined, thousands of pounds of pressure come down on the horses' ankles as they reach speeds of nearly forty miles per hour. Good nutrition from grazing was essential, and thoroughbreds found exactly that in the grasses of the region.

The bluegrass, *Poa pratensis*, grown lush and thick over the Inner Bluegrass limestone karst landscape, contained high amounts of calcium, extremely advantageous to young thoroughbreds, especially in the area of bone development and strength. No one is sure about the origins of this grass in Kentucky. Some believe it was imported from Eurasian cultures before white settlers arrived, while others believe the seed was brought by European colonists. It is a very common plant, found in most of Europe and northern Asia. Whatever the origin, the grass flourished in the region and became a central reason for the development of a distinctive thoroughbred culture. With the proliferation of thoroughbreds throughout the region, the style of racing began to change. In the early nineteenth century, quarter racing—short sprints down a narrow straightaway—gave way to grueling tests of endurance, usually four-mile heats, with the winner having to win two out of three. With the change in focus from blazing speed to tests of endurance, the breeding of horses changed as well. Breeders changed from breeding stocky speedballs to thoroughbreds.

Racing thoroughbreds and other breeds of horses was extremely popular among the upper class of the northern states. New York claimed to be the first state to boast the world's first dirt oval racetrack, built in 1821 (although a circular dirt track had already been established in Kentucky as early as the 1780s). This track, called the Union Course, hosted one of the great sporting events of the day, pitting the undefeated northern horse Eclipse against the great hope of the South, Sir Henry. A boisterous sixty thousand spectators showed up to watch the northern Eclipse prevail in the tiebreaking heat in a rousing sectional battle of equine athletes.

If horse racing was loved in the North, it was religion in the South. The gentleman class of the South took racing very seriously, and many duels were fought over suspected shenanigans. A gentleman's honor was imposed onto his horse. One possible shenanigan was the stealing of an opponent's goat. The goat was not just a stable mascot but also a calming presence to a high-strung racehorse. With the abduction, the upset thoroughbred would be unable to give his best effort at the track—hence the phrase "getting someone's goat" was born.

At first, "gentleman jockeys," usually the owners themselves, rode the horses in the contests, but in the mid-eighteenth century, enslaved African

Americans were used as jockeys. Some—like Cato, Austin Curtis and Simon—were so prolific that they were treated as the first sports heroes in America. Enslaved jockey Charles Stewart made so much prize money that he had an agent manage it.

As thoroughbreds crossed the mountains into Kentucky, racetracks naturally popped up across the landscape as well. One of the most popular was the first circular track in America, located between Crab Orchard and Stanford in Lincoln County. The track was built around a hill, and owner Colonel William Whitley, who also built the first brick house in Kentucky, called it Sportsman's Hill. Spectators climbed the hill at dawn for the August race meets and enjoyed a full view of the horses as they ran around it. Legend says that the American orientation of racing counterclockwise had its origins here. During the Revolution, Whitley ordered the races to be run counterclockwise because of the clockwise orientation of the British.

There is an egalitarian aspect of the circular track encircling a hill. Mainly, everyone could see. At the tracks in Europe, and to a certain extent in the eastern United States, the finish line was reserved for either the nobility or at least the elite, whose horses engaged in competition. On the frontier in southeastern Kentucky, with its more democratic attitudes, everyone was given a chance to see the action—even the finish of the race.

George Washington, Thomas Jefferson and later (and especially) Andrew Jackson enjoyed horse racing in various degrees of participation. All three were well known as excellent horsemen, in keeping with the country gentleman ideal they tried to emulate. Jefferson, as relayed by historian Edwin Morris Betts, wrote to his granddaughter in 1808, "Our races begin to-day but I am kept from them by an attack of rheumatism which came upon me in my sleep."[3] Jackson, upon winning the presidency in 1828, took prized thoroughbreds with him to Washington, D.C. He is commonly known to be the only United States president to run a racing stable out of the White House.

One of the most successful of the early thoroughbred breeders and owners in Kentucky was statesman Henry Clay. At his large estate, called Ashland, outside of Lexington, Clay began racing horses in 1808 and then breeding them in 1830. At some point, he even built a private racetrack on the property. Although as a Whig senator, Clay was deeply embroiled in the volatile issues of the day, he kept meticulous records of his horses, including foaling dates, race records, feedings and veterinary issues.

In 1806, Clay was part of a group that bought an aged thoroughbred stallion named Buzzard. Buzzard sired a broodmare, which then produced one of Clay's greatest runners, Woodpecker. Woodpecker was taken to

Henry Clay, statesman and thoroughbred breeder. *Courtesy of Ashland, the Henry Clay estate.*

Louisville in 1833 to run against the great Virginia horse Collier in a match race in four-mile heats. Clay's horse prevailed, to the delight of his many friends, furthering his status as a top-class horse breeder. Clay raced his horses mainly at tracks in the area, in Nashville, Louisville and Lexington.

Clay's Ashland stable included several horses that would prove influential for the breed. His mares Margaret Wood and Magnolia produced eleven future Kentucky Derby winners in their female tail lines. Magnolia was the grand dam of Iroquois, the first American-bred horse to win the English Derby in 1881. His stallion Yorkshire, given to him by United States naval officer Commodore Charles W. Morgan, produced many winners, evidently to the Clay family's surprise.

Clay, known as the "Great Compromiser," still liked to be right on the issues of the day. He also liked to be right about his horses. One can hear the "I told you so" in a letter to son James B. Clay in 1850:

> *John* [M. Clay] *won last week with the Glencoe filly by Yorkshire the Phoenix stake* [at Lexington], *and the next day he also won the two mile stakes with the Yorkshire colt from the Zhinghanie mare. I have not heard from home. You see that I did not judge so erroneously about Yorkshire.*[4]

Clay would be known as a respected thoroughbred breeder for years to come, but he had yet another connection to future generations of thoroughbreds. Little did Clay know that when he married Lucretia Hart in 1799 in a small house on her family's farm, called the Overton Farm, that same Lexington property would be purchased years later by horseman John Madden, founder of the future thoroughbred haven Hamburg Place.

While Henry Clay made his mark in politics in Washington, D.C., and his mark in thoroughbred racing in Kentucky, the rest of the Inner Bluegrass Region grew. Settlers came mainly to farm hemp and tobacco, with small towns beginning to connect in a maze of narrow dirt roads throughout the countryside. County governments were organized. Fayette and Bourbon Counties had already organized as counties as part of Virginia. Between 1792 and 1799, the Inner Bluegrass counties of Scott, Franklin, Harrison, Woodford and Jessamine were organized.

Small towns, some eventually becoming county seats of the Inner Bluegrass, sprang up along natural springs, rivers and crossroads. The earliest of these was Paris, settled on the Stoner Fork of the Licking River. Originally known as Hopewell while part of Virginia, in 1790 the name was changed to Paris to honor France's involvement in the American Revolution. Mary Todd, later first lady Mary Todd Lincoln, was born in Paris and lived there until she was fourteen, when she moved to Lexington. Today, Paris lies about seventeen miles northeast of Lexington, along the scenic Paris Pike, home to many beautiful and historic horse farms.

To the northwest, and forming the top of a triangle with Paris and Lexington, lies Georgetown, in Scott County. Georgetown was settled by a group of Baptists from Virginia led by Elijah Craig. The group settled alongside a natural spring they called Royal Spring. In 1790, the town of Georgetown was incorporated and would later be home to Georgetown College, an institution with its origins tracing to Craig and his group.

In 1786, the Virginia legislature designated one hundred acres of property owned by notorious General James Wilkinson to be set aside for a town. When Kentucky became a state in 1790, this town, called Frankfort, outbid several others in the region (including Lexington) to become the state capital. The first statehouse was built there in 1794.

Meanwhile, a contemporary of Henry Clay's began to establish himself as quite a successful horse breeder in the countryside just outside Lexington. He was a young doctor named Dr. Elisha Warfield. Warfield was only nine years old, and a part of the first influx of pioneers who settled in the Lexington area, when his family migrated from Maryland. His father opened a general store, but young Elisha Jr. was sent to Transylvania College in Lexington, a school founded in 1780 before Kentucky was even a state, eventually obtaining a degree in medicine.

After graduation, Dr. Warfield was not only a respected medical practitioner in the early years of Lexington but also a teacher. He later joined Transylvania's faculty as the first professor of surgery and obstetrics. Although always active in the community teaching and healing, Warfield was a sportsman deep down. To Warfield, nothing beat watching the pounding hooves of racing horses. He was a founding member of the Lexington Jockey Club, a group organized to improve the breed and to organize and conduct race meets.

Warfield, unlike most of his contemporaries, who were more interested in winning races, was greatly interested in thoroughbred bloodlines. He owned a copy of the English *General Stud Book* and was considered an expert on questions relating to thoroughbred pedigrees. He was probably the first in the Lexington community to advertise the breeding services of a stallion whose pedigree was listed in the English *General Stud Book*. Warfield listed the stallion named Tup for a stud fee of twenty-two dollars.

In 1821, Warfield's other business ventures necessitated an early retirement from medicine, but it's possible his motivation was that he wanted more time to devote to horses. In 1826, Warfield, along with his friend Henry Clay, was one of the founding members of the Kentucky Association for the Improvement of the Breeds of Stock, a group with similar goals as the Lexington Jockey Club. Several racetracks adorned Lexington already, but this group of horsemen built a track that would establish itself as the top racetrack in the area for over a century. This track, simply called the Association Track, was built on property adjacent to the Meadows, the name Warfield gave to the farm he bought the year before the track opened in 1828.

After Warfield's death in 1859, the Meadows Stud Farm, now sitting just outside the Lexington city limits, was bought by breeder Daniel Swigert, who owned the property for a time before purchasing Elmendorf Farm, located farther out on Paris Pike.

By 1903, a Lexington newspaper announced a sign of things to come for the old farm:

> *Mr. J. Eastern Keller, whose real estate projects fifteen or eighteen years ago had much to do with the awakening of Lexington in the latter 80's, and who recently returned here to take up residence has on foot the organization of a syndicate to purchase and subdivide The Meadows.*[5]

These plans never materialized, and the property was sold several more times before a post–World War II growth spurt finally sealed the old farm's fate. In 1945, the property was subdivided and replaced by the Meadows subdivision.

The farm was a bastion of pre–Civil War horse racing in the Bluegrass Region. Many great thoroughbreds were produced at the farm, and Dr. Warfield's community involvement and investment contributed volumes to early Lexington culture. But on March 29, 1850, a horse was born at the Meadows whose impact would forever change thoroughbred racing and stamp the region as the thoroughbred capital of the world. He would later be named Darley, and Darley would be renamed Lexington, the greatest sire in thoroughbred racing history.

## 2

# WOODBURN FARM AND
# THE CIVIL WAR

The Kentucky Horse Park is a true Kentucky gem and a horse lover's dream. Over twelve hundred acres of bluegrass await the visitor, with about 115 horses representing approximately thirty different breeds. Opened in 1978, visitors can peruse the park at their leisure and get to know, and sometimes even pet, many of the equine talent on display. The Hall of Champions features equine athletes that have achieved great things on the track or in the show ring. Visitors can pay their respects to several equine champions buried at the park, including Man o' War, and his greatest son, Triple Crown–winner War Admiral. The great African American jockey Isaac Murphy is buried at the entrance to the park as well.

Also on the grounds at the Kentucky Horse Park is a museum called the International Museum of the Horse. Here, one can learn about the horse's place in history, with fascinating exhibits showcasing horses from ancient times to the modern day. In 2010, this museum put on display a skeleton of a nineteenth-century thoroughbred named Lexington. The exhibit was a minor miracle; the horse had been in Smithsonian Institution storage for much of the time since his passing in 1875. For years, efforts were made to bring Lexington home, but to no avail. Finally, overcoming bureaucracy and red tape, Lexington came back to the Bluegrass, which is fitting because he, more than any other horse, revolutionized the thoroughbred breed and symbolized the dominance of the Kentucky-bred thoroughbred in the nineteenth century.

The skeleton of Lexington, the most influential American thoroughbred sire. *Courtesy of the Kentucky Horse Park, International Museum of the Horse.*

Lexington, originally called Darley, was born on Dr. Elisha Warfield's farm, the Meadow, on March 17, 1850. His bloodline was outstanding. He was sired by Boston, a winner of forty out of forty-five starts and the leading American sire from 1851 to 1853, and was out of the dam Alice Carneal, said to be a fast but nervous mare with an impeccable bloodline. The blood bay horse grew to just under sixteen hands, with excellent conformation and, unlike his sire and dam, a gentle and calm disposition.

Darley only raced in the colors of Dr. Warfield twice, although the horse was under lease to Warfield's black trainer, Henry Brown, due to the doctor's advanced age. The talented colt made his debut in the Association Stakes at Lexington as a three-year-old. He won easily and then followed up the win four days later with another victory at the Association Track, within shouting distance of Warfield's mansion at the Meadows. Between heats of the Citizens' Stakes, a syndicate led by prominent horsemen Richard Ten Broeck and Willa Viley made an offer to Dr. Warfield for the horse, and the price was accepted.

The future great horse's life almost ended soon after. He gained access to a store of field corn and tied up, resulting in an emergency treatment called "bleeding." This probably saved his life, although his training regimen was interrupted. That December, despite the setback, he easily won a match race in two heats against the filly Sallie Waters.

The syndicate sent Lexington, as he was now called, to compete in the Great Post Stakes in New Orleans. The colt won again but was much challenged by a horse named Lecomte, also a son of Boston. After this win, Ten Broeck bought out the rest of the syndicate for $5,000, determined to have full control over the talented horse. Ten Broeck may have wished he hadn't done so at the rematch with Lecomte a week later.

Here, Lexington met an extremely sharp Lecomte, which smashed a world record for the four-mile heat, defeating Lexington soundly. The next heat would prove equally as decisive, and Lexington left New Orleans with his luster worn. He was shipped to both New York and New Jersey but never raced due to several mishaps and bad luck. Finally returning to Natchez, Mississippi, Ten Broeck readied Lexington for a final match against his nemesis Lecomte in New Orleans. The final match between the two ended in disappointment for many, as it was known that Lecomte was recovering from a bout with colic and was probably not at full strength. Lexington won the first heat easily and won the match overall when Lecomte's owner forfeited the second heat.

During his second stint in New Orleans, Lexington's eyesight began to fail. Ten Broeck retired his horse as the third leading money earner of the day; his six wins in seven starts had earned $56,600. Ten Broeck sent the horse to John Harper's Nantura Stud near Midway, Kentucky, to begin his stallion career. Ten Broeck, obviously impressed with the rival Lecomte, purchased that horse for $10,000 and sent the horse to England, where the horse made only one start, finishing last. Ten Broeck's recent purchase was plagued by bouts of colic and leg injuries, making him only a shell of his former self. The great rival of Lexington died soon after.

Ten Broeck stood the promising young sire for two years at Nantura before interest from a Bluegrass neighbor proved to be an offer he couldn't turn down. The neighbor's name was Robert Aitcheson Alexander, owner of the Woodburn Farm. Alexander, having spent several years in Europe studying animal breeding genetics (although it wasn't called that at the time) and husbandry, knew exactly what kind of horse he was looking for and paid what was considered a record sum, $15,000 for the unproven and nearly blind stallion.

He certainly had no trouble with the cost. Robert Aitcheson (R.A.) Alexander was born into wealth in 1819 in Frankfort. Educated at Trinity College at Cambridge, he returned to Kentucky in 1851. While in England, his uncle, the holder of the vast Airdrie Estates in Scotland, passed away, making R.A. the beneficiary. He retained British citizenship to keep the estate, which earned him about $100,000 per year, mainly from the Black Band iron ore produced at the furnaces at that location.

Soon after returning to Kentucky, young Alexander started an iron-producing business venture in Muhlenberg County, Kentucky, along the Green River. It was his intention to bring the experienced and hardworking Scottish ironworkers to Kentucky to make a new life. They not only made a new life, but they also made a new town at the site of the furnaces. They called it Airdrie, after the former site in Scotland. Alexander invested about $350,000 in the venture and bought about seventeen thousand acres of mostly heavily forested land in western Kentucky.

It was quite a different world, the heavily forested backcountry of Muhlenberg County compared to the gentility of Scotland, for the aristocratic landowner. Although his employees called him "Lord Alexander" or "the lord," Alexander was known as quiet, modest and unassuming and preferred to be called "Mister." This probably caused confusion on more than one occasion in the wilderness of western Kentucky. As legend has it, one day an American backwoodsman named Williams encountered Alexander and was surprised at the appearance of the man before him. After looking Alexander over from head to toe, the man exclaimed, "So you are the lord are you? By gum, you are nuthin' but a human bein' after all, and a plain, ordinary, say-little sort of a feller at that. They said you was a Big Bug, but five foot six will reach you any day of the week, by Washington!"[6] Supposedly, Alexander was amused by the description.

Unfortunately, the furnaces never produced the desired amount of iron, and the venture was abandoned in 1857, after only two years of operation. General Don Carlos Buell of Civil War fame bought the property and lived there a number of years, first searching for oil fields and finally settling for coal. Buell died in the area in 1898.

There is no Airdire in Muhlenberg County today. In a 1913 account of the land, it was noted that "all of Airdrie's 25 frame houses or more have been abandoned" and "no trace of the buildings that stood on Airdrie Hill can be found."[7] Alexander's focus was no longer on producing iron but in the Bluegrass county of Woodford, where he began putting together the pieces of a wildly successful breeding farm.

Little did he know at the time, but he largely established the success of his farm with the purchase of one horse: Lexington. In June 1856, Alexander traveled to England with the intention of securing top European bloodstock. His advisor, Nelson Dudley, persuaded Alexander to track down Ten Broeck, who was also in England at the time, and said that "whatever else he bought, he must not leave England until he purchased Lexington,"[8] which was still back at Nantura Farm in Kentucky. That he did, and upon returning to Kentucky, Lexington made the short trip from Nantura Farm to Woodburn, where he would join the stallion Scythian, purchased on the trip to England, to embark on their Woodburn breeding careers.

Alexander studied pedigrees and applied scientific methods to breeding, whether it was cattle, sheep, pigs or horses. He constantly evaluated his farm; drainage, soil fertility, forestry and nutrition all played parts in his everyday decision-making. He looked to get the most out of Woodburn not by chance but by knowledge. He was from the same mold as Thomas Jefferson, minus the political ambitions—a landed country gentleman, deeply interested in the world around him, whether it was science or the arts. Also like Jefferson, Alexander loved racing horses.

Alexander brought in—or rather bought—some of the best equine minds of the times—slaves. About 1858, Alexander bought a seven-year-old slave named Ed Brown. Working as a groom and later as a jockey, Brown would become one of the foremost turf authorities in America. Later in life, Brown would win the Belmont Stakes as a jockey and then capture the 1877 Kentucky Derby as a trainer. Brown was not the only exceptional horseman at Woodburn. During the Civil War, Alexander bought Ansel Williamson, a great trainer of thoroughbreds who was put in charge of managing Alexander's racing stable. After the war, Williamson would be employed as noted horseman H.P. McGrath's trainer and immortalized forever as the first trainer to win the inaugural Kentucky Derby.

It soon became very apparent that the sons and daughters of Lexington could run faster, at longer distances, than other horses. Years later, it was also apparent that his grandsons and granddaughters could do the same. He was America's leading sire every year from 1861 to 1874 and then again in 1876 and 1878. He sired two of his best in 1861, the undefeated Asteroid and Norfolk. Supposedly, Alexander sold Norfolk for $15,001 because after he was ridiculed for spending so much on an unproven sire, "the day would come when he would sell one of the produce of the horse they despised [Lexington], for more money than he paid for the sire."[9] "The Blind Hero of Woodburn," as Lexington became known, continued his amazing run through the Civil War, until the war finally came to R.A. Alexander's doorstep.

When civil war finally erupted in 1861, after years of increased tensions over slavery, Kentucky wasn't sure what side to take. Governor Beriah Magoffin sympathized with the South, while the legislature was composed mainly of Unionists. President Lincoln sent Governor Magoffin a telegram early in the war requesting seventy-five thousand Kentucky troops, to which Magoffin wired back: "I will not send a man or a dollar for the wicked purpose of subduing my sister Southern states."[10] To the governor's dismay, many Kentucky young men did go off and fight for the North. To the governor's satisfaction, many more fought for the South. In the Bluegrass Region, with its main immigration coming from Southern states Virginia, Maryland and North Carolina and the predominance of large farming operations supported by slave labor, one would think the region would have been beholden to the Southern cause. But as R.A. Alexander saw the two sides take aim at each other, he and many like him in the region viewed the war as a disaster for the nation.

In a revealing letter to his sister Mary, written in May 1861, Alexander confides that "political affairs are so gloomy…it is enough to make one heartsick" and "is a matter of impossibility to discard them from one's mind. [Kentucky] is attempting to maintain a neutral position," but that neutrality would be honored by the Federal government only if Kentucky maintained neutrality—a very difficult thing to do with Governor Magoffin's Southern leanings. Alexander continued, "Such a course would make Kentuck(y) one of the greatest battlefields that the world ever saw."[11]

As it turned out, Alexander was wrong, although the state was strategically important enough for Lincoln to declare, "I hope to have God on my side, but I must have Kentucky." To be sure, there were skirmishes all over the commonwealth, including several within the Inner Bluegrass Region. The two largest battles were at Mill Springs, near Somerset, where in 1862 a Federal force pushed the Confederate force back into Tennessee, resulting in 164 dead on both sides. Later that year, the two sides engaged at Perryville, just west of the Bluegrass Region, where the Union army attempted to cut off Braxton Bragg's Confederate invasion into Kentucky. Almost 1,400 were killed on both sides; the South claimed victory, but the invasion throttled.

Alexander began making evacuation plans for his valuable equine livestock just months after writing the letter to his sister. Farms in the region always had to be on guard against cavalries from both armies, which desired the athleticism and soundness of Bluegrass horses. He traveled by railway to

Chicago, making several side trips to a community called Illiopolis, located almost dead center in Illinois. His foresight would be rewarded, although this was several years down the road.

Thoroughbreds were held in high regard, although many cavalrymen preferred standardbreds, still prevalent in the region and many bred at Woodburn Farm. Confederate general Basil Duke praised the standardbred breed as superior due to "his superior powers of endurance" and "his smoother actions and easier gaits," and maybe best of all, "his intelligence and courage make him more reliable in the field."[12]

Several farms in the region experienced raids on their bloodstock, sending farm owners scrambling for protection. Alexander, still officially a British subject, may have saved Woodburn from Confederate raids in the early years. Great Britain, because of its reliance on Southern cotton markets, sympathized with the South, although it maintained neutrality throughout the conflict. Legend says, although probably false, that Alexander flew the English flag at Woodburn during the early years of the war in hopes of being bypassed by the marauding Southern army. It must have worked to an extent because several Bluegrass neighbors sent horses to Woodburn to weather the storm.

After the Battle of Perryville in October 1862, Confederate forces withdrew to Tennessee. But throughout the three years until hostilities ended, Kentucky citizens endured raids led by armed guerrillas looking to wreak havoc—looting homes, burning bridges, destroying county courthouses and stealing horses. The Inner Bluegrass Region was a prime target for these raiders, and Woodburn Farm, with its barns full of the fastest horses in the area, would not escape this time.

As R.A. Alexander ate his midday meal on a warm summer afternoon in 1864, he received word that there was commotion at the stables. Notorious guerilla Jerome Clark, who many believed to be the bandit Sue Mundy, along with five other men, was the cause of the commotion, stealing five thoroughbreds, all sons of Lexington. Mundy himself stole the big prize: the undefeated racehorse Asteroid. By the time Alexander and several of his employees got to the barn, the thieves were gone. Alexander and his men raced to catch up and did so about ten miles away at the Kentucky River. Outnumbering the thieves, shots were exchanged, with Alexander and his men getting the upper hand. Several of the horses were recovered, but guerilla leader Mundy plunged Asteroid into the Kentucky River among the flying bullets and escaped.

There are several conflicting accounts of what happened next. Determined to get his prized horse back, Alexander asked a neighbor, Major Warren

Viley, to "undertake the thing for me" and "to ransom the colt for any price."
Viley took along two other men, both former Confederate soldiers, to help
in the dangerous operation. (One of the men was Ezekiel Clay, who would
later found Runnymede Farm.) In one account, the "gentlemen met two of
the scoundrels lagging behind and took Asteroid back at gunpoint."[13]

The other, more widely accepted account has Viley confronting Mundy,
requesting that he give the horse back, as it was a pet. Mundy refused, saying
the horse was "the best he ever rode."[14] Mundy was a good raider but a terrible
businessman. Not knowing the worth of the great racehorse, Mundy only
asked for the value of the horse he had previously ridden, worth $250, and a
mount to replace Asteroid. A deal was made, and Viley took Asteroid home
to Woodburn, accepting the cheers and congratulations of his neighbors but
not accepting any monetary reward from a grateful Alexander.

The excitement was short-lived. In the early evening of November 1, Sue
Mundy and his men paid Major Viley a visit at his Stonewall Farm, looking to
receive the horse that was promised as part of the ransom. They may have also
planned another raid on Woodburn, but Alexander was ready, arming his men
and placing lookouts around the property. Mundy skipped Woodburn this time.

Instead, his gang surrounded neighbor John Harper's Nantura Farm,
the farm where Lexington stood his first two years at stud. The pro-Union
Harpers had fought off an earlier attempt to ransack their farm and were
just as determined this time. In a heavy exchange of gunfire, Adam Harper,
the farm owner's brother, was fatally shot.

As the Civil War entered its final year, the region experienced a sharp
decline in order, as lawless bands of guerillas terrorized the countryside.
Coldblooded murders, followed by Federal retaliatory executions, became
commonplace. Sue Mundy remained at large. However, there was coming
to Kentucky a man whose fighting tactics and appetite for violence made
Mundy's group pale in comparison. This man was William Clarke Quantrill,
along with a band of 48 followers that included Frank and Jesse James.
Quantrill's reputation stemmed from an 1863 incident in Lawrence, Kansas.
Quantrill and his men captured 183 men and boys and then massacred them
in front of their families before torching the town.

Now this same Quantrill was in Kentucky. By mid-January, Quantrill and
Mundy's forces had joined together, raiding, pillaging and murdering all
over the region. Federal authorities pursued but had little success, seemingly
always several steps behind the guerrillas. The group's prime target was the
capture of horses. On February 2, the guerillas sped into Woodford County,
and once again their destination was Woodburn Farm.

Alexander knew that the farm was a target; he received an anonymous letter in mid-January warning that kidnapping for ransom money was in the works. In the early evening of February 2, what appeared to be Federal-uniformed soldiers came to the door, first demanding provender for two hundred horses and then changing their tune to the impressment of horses. Alexander asked to see their orders, only to be threatened at gunpoint. Alexander realized it was many of the same men who had visited his farm during the first raid. It is probable that both Sue Mundy and Quantrill participated, and Mundy was determined to get back "the best horse he ever rode." If Alexander put up resistance, the guerillas had a bargaining chip. Before visiting Woodburn, they had stopped at another farm to steal a horse and take a hostage. This hostage was the seventy-seven-year-old father of Major Viley, who had helped secure the ransom for Asteroid. Over the next hour, action took place all over the farm. At one point, Alexander himself scuffled with one of the marauders in his kitchen and managed somehow to pin the man and then push him out before bolting the doors.

While this was going on, the stables were plundered. Despite pleas that money, instead of horses, could be had, Quantrill's men would not be denied this valuable horseflesh. Quantrill himself was offered $10,000 not to take the great trotter Bay Chief, but he refused. They left Woodburn that evening with sixteen valuable horses. Although devastating, Alexander was fortunate in several regards. Violence threatened to erupt several times, but except for Alexander's minor kitchen scuffle, no shots were fired. Considering Quantrill's history, this was no minor achievement. Lexington remained safe, as his blindness proved to be a godsend in this case. His son Asteroid, the object of Sue Mundy's desires, would surely have been stolen again if not for the quick thinking of slave trainer Ansel Williamson.

With pistols drawn, guerillas demanded that Asteroid be brought out of his stall. At gunpoint, Williamson felt no need to argue and did what he was told. Only the horse he brought out wasn't Asteroid. In the darkness, the mistake wasn't caught, and the raiders rode off without the prized thoroughbred.

Within a year, Williamson would be a free man. He elected to remain at Woodburn and continue training horses before he went to work for Hal Price McGrath.

Quantrill and Mundy's group sped toward Midway, several miles down the dirt road. The elderly hostage, Willa Viley, exhausted from the events and the ride, fell from his horse and was left for dead in the cold November night. He was found alive and taken to his son's Stonewall Farm. He never recovered and died that March due to the exposure of that ride.

The small town of Midway was next on Quantrill's list. To slow pursuit of Federal forces in the area, Quantrill's guerillas torched the Midway telegraph office and train depot. Several citizens were robbed in the street before the guerillas, on their stolen horses, sped off again into the night.

For the next few months, the guerrillas were constantly on the move, evading Federal troops. At some point, the group split into several smaller units. On February 3, a group of Woodford County Home Guards surprised the small group that Quantrill led and nearly ended his notorious career. Just outside Lawrenceburg, Quantrill tried to escape the ambush, but his stolen horse, the great trotter Bay Chief, was shot several times. Quantrill managed to escape on the stricken animal but was overtaken when his wounded horse gave out. The great trotter died of his wounds ten days later, a great blow to Alexander. The wily Quantrill eluded capture by jumping onto another horse and speeding off into the woods. But Quantrill's fortune would not hold out much longer. In May of that year, he was tracked to a Spencer County farm and was severely wounded in a gunfight. He died a month later in Louisville, ending the life of one of the most notorious outlaws of the era.

Mundy was already dead by this time. He and a few of his men had made it as far as Breckenridge County when the gang split up in February, but they surrendered to Federal authorities after being trapped in a barn. Mundy was taken to Louisville and hanged on March 15 in front of a crowd of about ten thousand. The twenty-year-old Mundy was actually Jerome Clark; the name Mundy was invented by a Louisville newspaperman in a campaign against the military ruler in Kentucky. The name and legend stuck, and the name Sue Mundy still inspires tales and legends of that lawless time in Kentucky history.

In the month between Mundy's execution and Quantrill's capture, the Civil War ended. On April 9, 1865, Generals Ulysses S. Grant and Robert E. Lee met at Appomattox Court House in Virginia to set peace terms. Woodburn Farm's presence was there, as Grant rode in on a seventeen-hand thoroughbred named Cincinnati, a son of Lexington. The horse was given to Grant in 1863 as a gift from a dying man and quickly became a favorite of Grant's, who said it was "the finest horse he had ever seen."[15] He was so protective of the horse that he allowed only two other people to mount it—Admiral David Ammen, who had saved Grant's life as a child, and President Lincoln.

Several of the horses stolen by Quantrill's raiders were recovered. Despite great efforts to save the great trotter Bay Chief, which had been shot, he died of his wounds ten days later. Alexander's other great trotter, Abdullah, perished as well, probably from pneumonia after the overheated horse plunged into icy waters during an escape and then ran hard for several miles afterward.

After the second raid, Alexander was determined to evacuate his valuable bloodstock, although by this point it was probably too little, too late. In February 1865, Alexander shipped forty-two standardbred horses to Montgomery, Illinois, on land he purchased in 1863. In April, many of his thoroughbreds made the exodus to Williamsville, Illinois. It was reported that Lexington did not go freely: "The stallion refused to enter the train on his own accord, and slaves finally had to surround the raging, screaming stallion and literally lift him into the boxcar."[16]

The Bluegrass Region slowly returned to normal in the summer of 1865, minus the scourge of slavery. The effect of the Civil War on Kentucky's horse industry was devastating. It is estimated that there were ninety thousand fewer horses in Kentucky than when the war began in 1861. Alexander began to race his horses extensively after the war, but most thoroughbred owners did not have the resources or bloodstock Alexander did. Recovery for breeders lagged all over the Bluegrass Region as Alexander brought his horses back from Illinois. Over one hundred total horses were either shipped back to Woodburn or to racetracks in the region to resume their racing careers.

Lexington continued to dominate the breeding world; in 1866, his sons and daughters won an astounding 112 races. In upstate New York at the Saratoga Racecourse, a new stakes race called the Travers developed into a major attraction for horse owners. In the first fifteen runnings of the race, nine of the winners were sons and daughters of Lexington. Three Preakness Stakes winners, run at Pimlico Race Course in Maryland, were sired by the "Blind Hero of Woodburn." The Kentucky Derby, still about a decade from its founding, would be dominated by Lexington blood—six grandsons won the Louisville classic.

After the war, friends and acquaintances noticed a change in Alexander. Always small in stature, Alexander was known for his vast amount of energy. Due to the stresses caused by the war—no doubt at least in part due to the two Woodburn raids—his health deteriorated quickly. On December 1, 1867, the great breeder and master of Woodburn Farm died in his home. According to racing historian Robert Wooley, he did "more to improve the Kentucky thoroughbred and towards finding out causes and effects in the breeding problem than all of his contemporaries combined."[17]

Woodburn Farm was inherited by R.A. Alexander's brother, Alexander John (A.J.) Alexander, who moved into the large mansion on the property

Woodburn Mansion, home of A.J. Alexander, breeder of three Kentucky Derby winners. *Photo by author.*

that John Harper built in the 1840s. (R.A. never lived in this residence, preferring another residence, which no longer is standing. He made plans to build a grand mansion after the war, but those plans were never realized.) A.J. Alexander kept Dan Swigert on as the Woodburn racing manager, until Swigert struck out on his own and eventually founded the successful Elmendorf Farm. Swigert's brother-in-law, Lucas Brodhead, ran the stable successfully until 1893, when a great economic depression severely crippled the horse industry. Woodburn Farm dispersed its equine stock at the end of the nineteenth century, although the farm, today a part of Airdrie Farm, continues the thoroughbred breeding tradition.

Lexington died in July 1875, still a prolific sire in his later years. Even after his death, he led the North American sire rankings in 1876 and 1878. In announcing his death, the *New York Times* called him the "king of sires" and wrote that "Lexington founded a line of racehorses unequaled by the offspring of any other stallion in this country or England."[18] His remains were eventually donated to the Smithsonian Institution, where they remained in a box in storage for many years before coming home to Kentucky in 2010.

In the years following the Civil War, racing in the South was virtually nonexistent. The former Southern racing hotbeds of New Orleans and Nashville had little interest in racing, as reconstruction following the devastation of ruined farmland and torched cities were priorities in the post–Civil War South. Kentucky thoroughbred farms suffered as the demand for their products dwindled. A man in Louisville was determined to change this, and after several years of studying racing in Europe, he came home to help start the Louisville Jockey Club and Driving Park Association. His name was Meriwether Lewis Clark Jr., and the feature race he developed was patterned after the famous Epsom Derby. His race would be called the Kentucky Derby, and just a few months before the great Lexington died at Woodburn Farm, the first Kentucky Derby was held in Louisville. The question was: could the Kentucky Derby help rekindle a struggling thoroughbred industry in the Bluegrass Region?

# 3

# MERIWETHER LEWIS CLARK

# AND THE FIRST

# KENTUCKY DERBY

Meriwether Lewis Clark was a perfectionist. That's what growing up a Clark would do to a man in Louisville in the mid- to late nineteenth century. Being a Clark, at least a Clark in this line of the family, meant that eyes were continually on you. Being a Clark meant you were held to a high social standard and always played by the rules. And most of all, being a Clark meant you were a cornerstone of the Louisville community.

That's how it was when your great-uncle George Rogers Clark was a revered Revolutionary War hero and, to top it off, widely credited as the founder of Louisville. Or when your grandfather was William Clark, also a national hero who co-led the famous Lewis and Clark Expedition to the Pacific. And to make sure everyone knew what stock you came from, there was the name. Evidently, Meriwether Lewis Clark Sr. accepted the fate he had been given. Evidence suggests that Meriwether Lewis Clark Jr.—or "Lutie," as he was known as a young man—did not.

Lutie's father married into a prominent Louisville family, the Churchills, in 1834. Lutie's mother, Abigail Prather Churchill, died when he was only six years old, prompting Clark Sr. to send Lutie off to live with his wealthy uncles, John and Henry Churchill. Clark attended St. Joseph College in nearby Bardstown and then worked as a teller at a bank. In 1871, he did as his father had done and married into wealth. His bride was Mary Martin Anderson, a young woman who had been raised by two aunts, one of whom was Pattie Anderson. Pattie Anderson was married to celebrated horseman

Meriwether Lewis Clark, founder
of the Kentucky Derby. *Courtesy of
the Kentucky Derby Museum.*

Richard Ten Broeck, the leader of the syndicate that purchased the young stallion Darley and changed his name to Lexington. Clark's wife not only had horse-racing connections, but she also soon inherited a vast fortune from a wealthy relative, making Clark independently wealthy as well.

Although Clark's Churchill uncles enjoyed racing thoroughbreds and were involved in Louisville groups promoting the sport, it was probably the influence of the effervescent Ten Broeck that lit young Clark's fire for horse racing. Louisville offered two tracks for thoroughbreds after the Civil War: Woodlawn and Greenland. Both were plagued by mismanagement, and both were out of business by 1870. The largest city in the commonwealth, with a population now over 100,000 people and located only miles away from the farms of the Inner Bluegrass Region, had no track to showcase the horses.

In 1872, a group of thoroughbred breeders met with the well-connected Clark to discuss ways a new track might be established in Louisville. Although members of Clark's family had racing in their backgrounds, Clark himself was unfamiliar with much of the business aspects of the sport. No doubt it was the Clark name, still holding a lot of influence and prestige, that made Lutie attractive to the horsemen. A trip to Europe opened Clark's eyes on how race meets should be conducted. Strict rules were enforced on the tracks, bookmakers were regulated and the European thoroughbred breeding industry closely watched to keep the breed "thoroughly bred." One race in particular, the Epsom Derby in England, attracted tens of thousands to see the top three-year-olds clash at a distance of a mile and a half. Clark witnessed the 1873 running alongside his uncle John Churchill. Certainly, a positive impression was made.

Clark met with prominent members of the English Jockey Club, and the seeds began to sprout of what racing should look like in Louisville. One horseman pressed Clark, "Why do you not start a jockey club at the metropolis of your state and have representative races? If your people appreciate them, others will do so. Give class races, and by your stakes compel the large establishments to breed for them."[19] The large establishments, of course, were the large thoroughbred farms struggling in the aftermath of the Civil War. Clark's idea was to pattern three main stakes races after English examples: the Epsom Oaks, a race for three-year-old fillies, would become the Kentucky Oaks; the English St. Leger Stakes, a race for three-year-old colts and fillies, would become the Clark Stakes (today the Clark Handicap); and the featured race, the Epsom Derby, would become the Kentucky Derby.

Clark returned to Louisville excited about this new opportunity to leave his stamp on his hometown. Could this thoroughbred racing venture propel Clark to elite status in Kentucky society? More importantly, could it lift him up in stature to, in his eyes, be worthy of his name? Upon returning to Louisville, Clark helped organize the Louisville Jockey Club and Driving Park Association. Several within the group believed Clark to be too young and inexperienced to lead the group, but the first choice as president resigned after only three months of service. A second member declined the offer, and Clark, the third choice, took over as president in October 1874. He plunged headfirst into his new role and was determined to make the track a success.

A one-mile oval racetrack was laid out in the fall of 1874 on John and Henry Churchill's property, about three miles south of downtown Louisville. The Churchills had farmed the property in the past, and a will from 1850 notes the property had a small family cemetery. Several weeks before its opening, a Louisville newspaper could barely contain its excitement:

*The inaugural meeting…will mark an important event in the city of Louisville. As the metropolis of the state which has produced the finest and fastest horses that have ever stepped upon the turf, Louisville ought to take the lead in other cities in racing matters.*

The writer continued to promote the race by imploring, "In England, 'Derby Day' is the greatest of all days, and it can be here if everybody will just say so."[20]

On a Monday afternoon, May 17, 1875, about ten thousand people said so. The crowd packed the freshly painted grandstand and clubhouse, with hundreds more crossing the track into the "inner field." The second race on the card was the main event—the Kentucky Derby—and fifteen horses went to the post to contest the mile-and-a-half distance. Thirteen of the fifteen jockeys were African American that day, and the field was dominated by Kentucky- bred horses from the Bluegrass Region. The first to cross the finish line was H.P. McGrath's Aristides, bred at one of the largest thoroughbred farms in the world at that time, McGrathiana.

The first Kentucky Derby did what it was designed to do—attract the best horses in the region to showcase the products of Bluegrass farms. Although the Derby would not attract top East Coast horses until the following year, the talent in the first Derby was significant. When McGrath's Aristides finished the mile and a half run in 2:37.75, it was the fastest clocking for a three-year-old at that distance anywhere in the United States. Aristides was fast, and he beat several other very good horses in the competitive field.

The original grandstand and clubhouse at Churchill Downs. *Courtesy of the Kentucky Derby Museum.*

Even the East Coast media, typically holding the western tracks as inferior (just after the Civil War, they usually were), were impressed by the talent assembled for the first Kentucky Derby. After rattling off the list of probable contenders, the *New York Times* commented:

> *The majority of these are winners this year, and the race is most important in determining the favorite for the great stakes at Jerome Park, Long Branch and Saratoga, where most of the above colts have engagements. The betting on the result last night showed the interest taken in the event.*[21]

Ironically, one of the horses not listed as one of the notables was the eventual winner, Aristides. But his day was coming.

H.P. McGrath's other Derby starter, Chesapeake, was considered the more talented colt in the barn. As a two-year-old, Chesapeake won important stakes races at Monmouth and Saratoga, and McGrath swore he would have won the prestigious Saratoga Cup, but the high-strung horse bolted the other way at the start and finished last. Another contender, Searcher, made headlines for running a mile in Lexington in 1:41.75, the fastest clocking for a mile at that time, in a race leading up to the Derby. The Derby distance proved too much for him, and he finished mid-pack. Ten Broeck, a horse named for the prominent turfman who had so much influence with Clark, ran fifth in the inaugural Derby but became a legend, smashing several long-distance running records afterward.

These were all horses hailing from the Bluegrass Region, making their mark not just in a regional setting but also on the national stage. Excitement for racing was beginning to build again in the still war-tattered South, as some of the fastest horses were not being sold and raced exclusively in the East but were staying home and racing in Kentucky.

One year later, the second Kentucky Derby had a much different feel from the first, but the enthusiasm for the quality of bloodstock was the same. Of course, Kentucky newspapers promoted the race with flowery adjectives, trying to boost public enthusiasm for the race. But once again, even the sometimes starchy *New York Times* was impressed: "The announcement of this brilliant field of starters for the first really great race of the year occasioned much excitement in the pool-rooms last night."[22] East Coast stables served notice, and the second Derby became an invasion of extremely wealthy stable owners. Wealthy New York businessman Pierre Lorillard sent his gelding Parole to Louisville, only to see him beaten by another gelding, Vagrant, owned by another New Yorker and business partner, William Astor.

Before the gelding was sold to Astor, he reeled off five victories in six starts as a two-year-old, stamping himself as a horse to be reckoned with. Vagrant won the Phoenix Hotel Stakes in Lexington for his three-year-old debut, before his owner and breeder, T.J. Nichols of Paris, Kentucky, sold the talented gelding. Astor opened up his substantial checkbook and bought the horse for $7,000 just two weeks before the Derby. Astor, in his first year of racing, experienced the ups and down of racing horses in the few weeks afterward. His newly purchased horse won the Kentucky Derby and then followed that with a second-place finish in the Clark Stakes. He shipped east and won a race in Philadelphia but then went lame soon after. The horse recovered but never regained his superior racing form. Finally back to the races as a five-year-old, the former Derby winner ran twelve times and couldn't finish first or second once.

Meriwether Lewis Clark must have felt very proud that his brand-new Louisville Jockey Club attracted such high-powered stables as Lorillard and Astor. Attendance was strong throughout the spring and fall race meets, and Clark followed up his business success with political success. He was elected councilman for Louisville's Fifth Ward. The Louisville Jockey Club became Clark's jockey club, and he put everything he had—both professional and personal—into making sure it was a success. Even the weather on Derby day had Clark's stamp: a sunny Derby was known as "Lew Clark's Luck," or simply a "Clark Day."[23]

It wouldn't last. Clark's extreme adherence to racing rules, and his forceful and direct way of enforcing them, made him popular with the public and newspaper editors but sometimes unpopular with horse owners and trainers. A troubling event in September 1879 may have been an ominous sign of things to come for Clark. Stable owner Captain Thomas G. Moore confronted Clark at Louisville's Galt House hotel, where Clark kept an office, demanding an apology for insulting him on the track. Clark replied that he would apologize personally but not publically. Both men ended up pulling guns, with Moore shooting Clark, wounding him severely. Clark recovered from the incident, and no charges were brought forth. Moore's only penalty was to be ruled off the turf. After a year, this ruling was overturned by Clark himself.

The Louisville Jockey Club, although struggling to break even on the business side, continued attracting the top horses of the day during the decade of the 1880s, exciting the racing public. Former New York butchers and now the powerful horse-owning brothers Phil and Mike Dwyer brought a grandson of Lexington named Hindoo to Louisville in 1881. Hindoo was the Secretariat of his day, dominating the competition, setting track speed records, winning thirty of thirty-five races and never finishing out of the money. His easy four-length victory in the seventh Kentucky Derby and subsequent wins in New Jersey, New York and Pennsylvania made a star out of not only Hindoo but also his sire Virgil back at Elmendorf Farm in the Bluegrass Region. Virgil would sire three Kentucky winners: Vagrant, Hindoo and Ben Ali.

Not only was the racing good at Clark's track but the social elements were outstanding as well. At the close of the fall race meet in 1882, the October 4 *Louisville Commercial* chimed that "it is doubtful whether in all the time and amongst the vast numbers in attendance there has been a single individual on the grounds grossly intoxicated. The absence of profanity was also a very striking feature."

Anyone who has ever been to a racetrack knows this was certainly a great exaggeration, as newspaper writers of the day were often prone to do. But the point is well taken: Clark worked incessantly to keep the Louisville Jockey's Club image, an extension of his image, intact. He also worked tirelessly on keeping the grounds comfortable for spectators, whether it was making sure the surrounding dirt roads were kept watered to keep the dust down or planning what today we would call green space around the outer edges of the property: "Clark is to buy west of the grounds some seventy acres, thus adding to the grounds a neat strip of woods and open fields. This will be converted into a driving park. A lake will be constructed along a low, marshy portion of the land."[24]

Most of the green space never materialized because the financial concerns of the Louisville Jockey Club were getting dire. Despite good intentions, good horses and good press, the Louisville Jockey Club looked as though it was going the way of every other track in Louisville—toward bankruptcy. Clark pumped his own money into the operation, but the track barely hung on. Then a public relations disaster struck in 1886 in the form of one of the wealthiest horse owners in the world, James Ben Ali Haggin.

Haggin was originally from Harrodsburg in the Bluegrass Region, but as a young man, he left to practice law in California. While there, he entered the mining business and eventually, along with several partners, achieved great wealth. A master at speculating in land, Haggin also loved to speculate on his horses. He entered a thoroughbred named for his son, Ben Ali, in the 1886 Kentucky Derby, but just days before, a dispute over bookmaking rights caused the wealthy owner much consternation. Irate that he didn't have access to bookmakers to back his horse, he threatened to pull his entire stable from the track's grounds. A boisterous retort from a Churchill Downs (as it was unofficially known by now) official got back to the powerful horse owner, and although Ben Ali won the Derby, Haggin made good on his word and left town with his horses the next day. Haggin's powerful influence dissuaded other owners from stabling horses at Churchill Downs. This episode marked a downturn in the quality of horses for several decades, and the financial situation for the track worsened.

Dissatisfied rumblings within the Louisville community kept Clark on edge, ready to defend his leadership within the organization. Historian Samuel Thomas recounts a letter from an unidentified stockholder from February 1890, listing complaints about Clark's business struggles:

> *I have no feeling against Col. M. Lewis Clark. He may be satisfied...but I don't think the public is at all satisfied. Any ordinary observer can see that racing at the Jockey Club course has been deteriorating year by year... Louisville is the metropolis of the greatest stock raising State in the Union. It ought to have a broad gauged Jockey Club run on business principles...for the thousands of people who love good racing and are willing to pay for it.*[25]

Clark worked feverishly to reverse this trend. Despite a few notable moments, the late 1880s and the early 1890s were disappointing, as other western races, like the Latonia Derby and especially Chicago's American Derby, overshadowed the Kentucky Derby. The 1891 Kentucky Derby proved to be a bizarre exhibition of racing and a great embarrassment for Clark, as he watched only four horses go to the post. Unknown to Clark, or to the gathered crowd, all four trainers had the same racing strategy. As the horses left the post, a stunned crowd watched as the four horses galloped slowly around the track, each jockey waiting for the other to move. All four jockeys had received instructions to let someone else set the pace and make a move toward the end. At the head of the stretch, all four took off, and Kingman proved to be the best sprinter. The damage was done—the race lasted almost three minutes, prompting the local newspapers to call the Derby a "race for dogs," likening the race to a "funeral procession." Clark's Derby dream was falling apart, as was his personal life.

In 1886, after years of devoting everything to the Jockey Club, at the expense of his family, Clark and his wife separated. Clark moved to where he felt most at home, inside the Churchill Downs clubhouse. His wife eventually moved to Paris, France, five years later. Clark's former athletic build turned to obesity, and health problems occurred as a result of the excess weight, diet, anxiety and gunshot wound. He turned to two things for comfort: alcohol and his work. His personality, always intense, turned irritable and volatile as depression took hold. By 1894, the Louisville Jockey Club was teetering on bankruptcy, and Henry Churchill, Clark's uncle and still a Jockey Club director, wished to "cut up the land and sell it as town lots."[26]

Instead, the track was sold to a new group called the New Louisville Jockey Club. Clark remained at the track, but only as a presiding judge, and was not involved with daily operations or management. Clark watched the new management make many changes at the track. First, a new grandstand, featuring twin spires, was built on the opposite side of the original grandstand. A lavish clubhouse was constructed soon after. In a bow to pressures of horseman, the Kentucky Derby distance was shortened a quarter mile. Eventually, these changes paid off.

In 1903, the track hired a Louisville tailor named Matt Winn, who did what Clark could not do. Under Winn's direction and guidance, the Kentucky Derby developed into the nation's premier horse race in the 1910s. Winn understood that for the Derby to be successful, it had to be more than a race. The Derby had to be an event, complete with celebrity involvement and traditions such as gold trophies and garlands of roses. Winn understood the sentimental attachment Kentuckians had to Bluegrass culture. Singing "My Old Kentucky Home" as the predominately Kentucky-bred thoroughbreds paraded in front of the twin spires proved to be that magical moment Winn desired. Matt Winn made the Kentucky Derby, *the* Derby.

The pressures of being Meriwether Lewis Clark Jr. finally took their toll on the founder of the Kentucky Derby in a tragic way. With both his personal life and business life in tatters, and the pressures he no doubt put on himself as the follower of so many other successful and legendary Clarks, he killed himself in a hotel room in Nashville. The perfectionist Clark could not cope with an imperfect ending.

Yet, the Kentucky Derby did exactly what it was designed to do. Churchill Downs, and especially its biggest race, the Kentucky Derby, were built to create a greater demand for the Kentucky thoroughbred. It worked when Clark was alive; from 1875 to 1899 (the year of his death), twenty-one of twenty-five Kentucky Derby winners came from Kentucky farms. R.A. Alexander's brother, A.J. Alexander, bred three Derby winners at recovering Woodburn Farm. Alexander's former racing manager Dan Swigert bred three more at his Elmendorf Farm. The first major challenge to Kentucky's thoroughbred industry was the devastation caused by the Civil War. In response, the formation of the Louisville Jockey Club and its feature race, the Kentucky Derby, solidified Kentucky's prominence as the birthplace of the fastest horses in the world.

# 4

# TWENTIETH-CENTURY

# CHALLENGES

*Anti-Gambling Reformers and Suburban Sprawl*

At the dawn of the twentieth century, the Bluegrass Region of Kentucky had established itself as the place in America to breed thoroughbred racehorses. Other regions, mainly in Tennessee, Maryland and Virginia, and later in Florida, all had prominent thoroughbred breeding farms, but it was the Inner Bluegrass Region of Kentucky that dominated the breeding landscape. A travel guidebook from 1905 confirms, "The one thing that makes the city [Lexington] of more than passing interest, is the fact that it is the metropolis of the famous Bluegrass Region which is in turn the center of the blooded horse interests of the country."[27] Tourists, both American and foreign, were already traveling to see the beauty of the region at such an early date. The guidebook touted James Haggin's Elmendorf Farm, James and Foxhall Keene's Castleton Stud and Milton Young's Coldstream Farm (formerly McGrathiana Farm), among others.

Thoroughbred breeders from all over the country bought land and relocated their stock to farms in the Bluegrass Region. Arthur Boyd Hancock, a breeder in Virginia, married into a Kentucky family and started Claiborne Farm in Bourbon County, outside the small town of Paris. Businessman and gambler E.R. Bradley came from Florida and founded the Idle Hour Stock Farm in 1906, while Payne Whitney arrived from New York to establish Greentree Stud in 1914. All these names became synonymous with breeding excellence, along with Warren Wright's Calumet Farm, founded a decade later in 1924, and further cemented Kentucky's dominance in the thoroughbred breeding industry worldwide. Kentucky thoroughbred breeding farms now supplied the majority of horses in stables, from the up-and-coming western tracks in California to the midwestern tracks in Chicago and St. Louis to the powerful eastern stables in Maryland and New York. By 1897, roughly 314 racetracks dotted the American landscape. The demand for thoroughbreds ensured a booming breeding economy.

But storm clouds were forming on the horizon. While no other state or region could challenge Kentucky's dominance on the industry of breeding fast thoroughbreds, another foe emerged to derail, or even destroy, the industry. The late nineteenth century ushered in the "Age of Reform," also known as the Progressive era. This reactionary movement, stemming from the unrest caused by massive industrial growth and widespread political corruption, attempted to cure the ills of society. The movement delved into almost all areas of social and political life, gaining traction at all levels of government from about 1890 to 1920. Among the victories counted by the Progressives were the Eighteenth Amendment, prohibiting the sale and manufacture of alcohol; women's suffrage; and, eventually, a war against America's thoroughbred racetracks. The movement proved devastating. By 1908, only 25 racetracks survived. In just eleven years, 289 racetracks across the nations closed their doors.

To the Progressives, racing the horses was not the issue; gambling on them was. A common belief among Progressives was that government should play a role in solving social problems and fairness in economic matters was paramount in establishing a more just America. It was here that the reformers took aim at the thoroughbred industry.

For years, racetracks constantly fought against the perception that big-money interests controlled the results at the finish line. Bookmaking was the preferred form of gambling, and racetracks facilitated and encouraged bookmakers to make it easy for racing patrons to gamble. Unfortunately, bookmaking also remained largely unregulated and susceptible to inside information, fixed races and eventually public indignation. "For many years past…the atmosphere had been rife with rumors of conspiracies between jockeys, trainers, and bookmakers pre-arranging the results of races in fraud of the public."[28] To make matters worse, many bookmakers also served as owners, trainers and racetrack management, the very people in charge of regulating the sport. When those roles intertwined, it was usually the betting public that was left behind.

Despite public wariness of "the fixes," thoroughbred racing continued to draw huge crowds all over the country, surpassed in popularity only by baseball on the American sporting landscape. But Kentucky breeders looked on with concern as the reform movement began to gather steam against the industry. New Jersey became one of the first casualties and closed its tracks in 1898. Chicago's tracks, including the resplendent Washington Park, home to the prestigious American Derby, closed in 1905. The Tennessee General Assembly passed an anti-gambling law that closed its racetracks in 1906; they would never reopen. California followed, closing all racetracks within its borders in 1909.

The biggest blow to the thoroughbred breeding economy was yet to come. In 1911, thoroughbred racing took the biggest punch the reformers had to throw: New York, with its seven major racetracks, closed its gates due to Progressive-era reforms. Although the ban was lifted just two years later, New York racing struggled, at first, to restore its place as the top city in America for horse racing. All three tracks in Brooklyn—Brighton Beach, Gravesend and Sheepshead Bay—closed their doors, never to reopen for horse racing again. The remaining tracks after the ban—Jamaica, Aqueduct and Belmont, along with Saratoga in upstate—reestablished New York as the top racing state during the early twentieth century.

Kentucky, home at this time to the finest thoroughbred farms in the world, as well as Churchill Downs, whose Kentucky Derby was gaining momentum as the premier horse race in America, did not escape the aim of the anti-gambling establishment. In 1906, to combat the anti-racing groups, the Kentucky General Assembly formed the first state-run racing commission in America to ensure that racing within its borders was legitimate and not a corrupt system enriching bookmakers and gamblers off fixed races. The commission, almost immediately, banned all bookmaking, replacing this form of wagering with the easier-scrutinized parimutuel system. The parimutuel system, a system of wagering invented in France in 1867 (*parimutuel* means "among ourselves"), pools the money wagered, with the track taking a percentage, usually about 20 percent, and then paying out according to odds determined by the betting public. Parimutuel wagers were also easily taxed, a fact that softened the public's stance on gambling.

The public was reminded and reassured constantly that racing was fair and legitimate. On May 3, 1906, the *Louisville Times* promoted the safety and legitimacy of the racetrack for the upcoming Derby Day. "Captain Jim Jacobs is in charge of the police at the Downs, and as usual, is discharging his duties to perfection," and "Chief of Detectives Tom Maher and his men issued skidoo tickets to the touts and suspects in general. Peggy Humble, the old Pinkerton man, who knows every racetrack crook in the country, did splendid work." Later that year, the same newspaper, at the conclusion of the fall race meet on October 15, commented in a relieved tone that "the game here has been free from scandal."

That same year, an episode at Churchill Downs further cemented the need for regulation and order. Amid rumors of race fixing, two rival bookmakers, Steve L'Hommodieu and Jim Davis, almost came to blows after a heated exchange of words and threats over a payment issue. The newspaper clearly sided with the local bookie Davis by declaring, "Davis finished first in the word argument," and after looking L'Hommodieu "squarely in the eye," nothing resulted.[29] The following year, L'Hommodieu's troubles mounted. Already banned from eastern racetracks, and under suspicion at the western ones, he allegedly attempted to bribe jockey W. Fischer at Churchill Downs, resulting in a ban for life by the Louisville Jockey Club.

L'Hommodieu was clearly the type of character that racetracks sought to avoid, but without heavily regulated gambling laws, they found it difficult to do so. L'Hommodieu was a known "plunger," one who gambled huge sums of money, and in 1900, the *New York Times* listed L'Hommodieu as one of the three most successful gamblers in the country, although "he won so many bets, under such remarkable conditions, that early last season his operations became the subject of scandal." Although forced to officially "retire" from the tracks, he nevertheless "is still known to speculate heavily through commissioners, who place bets for him at the track and poolrooms."[30] L'Hommodieu was just one of many gamblers at that time who knew how to circumvent and profit off the loose and freewheeling style of gambling that bookmaking allowed.

Despite the formation of the Kentucky Racing Commission in 1906, anti-gambling crusaders were not mollified and fought to shut down all thoroughbred racetracks within the borders. Although the reformers were able to weaken the bite of the mint julep through the prohibition of alcohol, closing down racing for good in a state like Kentucky proved futile—especially since the Kentucky Derby was coming into its own and was regarded as the top race in America. The efforts, led by a Protestant group called the Churchmen's Federation, continued into the 1920s. One major advantage Kentucky enjoyed was that many state politicians in Frankfort had personal, political and economic ties to the horse industry, cementing its protection against the anti-gambling forces that had destroyed racing in other states.

Kentucky breeders, however, were in a quandary. Without a thriving national racing industry, there could be no thriving Kentucky breeding industry. The national demand for thoroughbreds diminished, so breeders were forced to reduce their thoroughbred bloodstock in favor of cattle, sheep and poultry. As one Derby historian noted, "By 1911, it was more profitable to ship mares to Australia, than to auction them in Lexington."[31] Breeders looked to other markets to sell horses in far-off places such as England, France, Russia and even South America with mixed success. England, in order to protect the economic interests of its own thoroughbred breeders, responded with the devastating Jersey Act in 1913. This act restricted England's *General Stud Book* to horses whose bloodlines were already registered in the studbook, eliminating most American thoroughbreds' inclusion.

It was estimated that from 1908 to 1913, about fifteen hundred thoroughbreds were shipped overseas, most of which would never return. One of the greatest racehorses of the American turf, Colin, was one of these, shipped to England in 1908. Although undefeated in fifteen starts and named Horse of the Year in 1907 and 1908, English breeders shunned him due to his "half-breed" bloodlines. Colin eventually returned to America and died on a farm in Virginia in 1932.

In February 1908, Kentucky breeders gathered in Lexington to discuss how to fight the New York anti-gambling bill, known as the Hart-Agnew Bill. Not only were they concerned about loss of revenue on bloodstock, but also property values in the Bluegrass Region plummeted 25 to 50 percent. A committee of three was chosen—Major Thomas B. Carson, Charles H. Berryman and Colonel Milton Young—and they in turn nominated Major P.P. Johnston of the National Trotting Association to appeal to New York legislators in an attempt to either amend or overturn the law. This proved unsuccessful, as there was no stopping the momentum of the reform movement. New York racing began its quick decline until it completely stopped in 1911.

Many thoroughbred breeders and owners in the Bluegrass Region could not survive the adverse business climate that the reform movement created. Bluegrass Region society gasped with the announcement that Edward Corrigan, owner of 1890 Kentucky Derby winner Riley and founder of Chicago's Hawthorne Racetrack, was leaving. Another to get out of the business was the ever-prominent Colonel Milton Young, owner of the resplendent McGrathiana Stud.

The reform movement's hold on the thoroughbred industry began to subside in the 1920s as tracks switched to the parimutuel form of gambling and the industry better regulated against fixed races. Despite the stock market crash of 1929, and the subsequent Great Depression that ravaged the country, Kentucky horse farms slowly rebounded economically. This was the time of the great thoroughbred heroes Man o' War, which lived as a celebrity on Faraway Farm outside of Lexington, and his son War Admiral, winner of the 1937 Triple Crown. Seabiscuit caught the public's imagination and beat War Admiral in the famous match race, continually making front-page headlines and captivating the public. Gallant Fox, Equipoise and Johnstown won big races and were made equine heroes. Like baseball, thoroughbred racing was as popular as ever, due to the exploits of these great horses. Sports also created an outlet and distraction from the economic hardships caused by the Depression. In addition, taxed parimutuel wagers contributed to the depleted state coffers during the Depression.

Several legendary Bluegrass farms were established at this time. Calumet Farm, although founded in 1924 as a standardbred breeding farm, established itself as a leading thoroughbred breeding operation in 1932. With its foundation sire Bull Lea, Calumet dominated thoroughbred breeding in America for decades, not only in Kentucky but also worldwide. Another successful farm, Greentree Farm, founded in 1926 by John Hay Whitney, produced many outstanding runners, including Kentucky Derby winners Twenty Grand (1931), Shut Out (1942) and 1953 Horse of the Year, Tom Fool.

Farms were not the only things popping up in the region during the Great Depression. In 1936, Keeneland Race Course opened just west of Lexington on property owned by breeder John Oliver (Jack) Keene, replacing the Kentucky Association track that closed in 1933. The track, originally a not-for-profit enterprise, showcased the equine talent bred, raised and trained on the farms in the community. In 1943, due to wartime travel restrictions, Keeneland hosted its first yearling sale. Prior to this, most yearlings were shipped to Saratoga in New York to be sold at auction, more convenient for wealthy East Coast buyers. Since 1943, the sales (currently, four sales are held throughout the year) have attracted buyers from all over the world, hoping to purchase either a future racing champion, a stallion prospect, a broodmare or all three.

The region continued its momentum in the decades following World War II as other prominent farms followed, either establishing themselves on previous farms or on undeveloped land. Gainesway, Spendthrift, Jonabell and Pin Oak, among many others, kept Kentucky at the forefront of thoroughbred breeding.

The Bluegrass Region not only attracted horsemen and horsewomen from all over the world to establish farms or to conduct business, but also the region became more and more popular as a tourism destination. As the national interstate system developed, and as the middle class had more and more money with which to travel and vacation, the commonwealth of Kentucky became a popular tourism destination. Tourists flocked to see the natural wonders of Mammoth Cave and the beauty of the Appalachian Mountains or to visit Hodgenville, the birthplace of Abraham Lincoln. An impressive state park system developed around natural wonders like Cumberland Falls or large man-made lakes such as Lake Cumberland. People also came to the Bluegrass Region to see its equine heroes and savor the rolling fields and picturesque farms, home to the fastest thoroughbreds in the world.

In the meantime, post–World War II America ushered in much social, economic and cultural change. The United States experienced the "baby boom," generally considered to range from 1946 to 1957, when a staggering 78.3 million Americans were born. In just twenty years, from 1940 to 1960, the United States' population grew from about 132 million people to about 180 million people. Also at this time, a combination of affordable automobiles and better roads made living outside of urban areas attractive for young families. Large cities across the nation began to lose population to the outlying housing developments that popped up outside of every metropolis. The term "white flight" was coined, as most blacks and other minorities were forced directly, or indirectly, to remain in the crumbling inner cities. Agents used such practices as "exclusionary covenants," referring to a practice that restricted sale of a property based on race, and "blockbusting," a real estate scheme in which a house in a neighborhood would be sold to a minority family with the intention of scaring the white population into believing their property would devalue greatly. These same agents profited off the exodus, as well as the reselling of the property to the incoming minority family.

Lexington, in the heart of the Bluegrass, was no different. In his *Bossism and Reform in a Southern City: Lexington, Kentucky, 1880–1940*, historian James Duane Bolin observed that Lexington's "white flight" at first followed streetcar lines, and later automobile routes, into the developing subdivisions at the fringes of the city limits. "Between 1910–1930, 65 percent of the increase in Lexington's white population found housing in outlying subdivisions."[32] At the same time, Lexington's African Americans resided mainly in the older inner-city districts. "Poor black neighborhoods," as described by Lexington reformers, like Chicago Bottom, Brucetown, Davis Bottom, Goodloetown, Yellmantown, Pralltown and Irishtown, had dwellings that were "so badly out of repair that they should be vacated, unless practically rebuilt."[33]

Although the term "suburb" is associated with the 1950s, it is a myth that suburbs were invented during post–World War II America. During the late nineteenth century, and especially true on the East Coast, interurban and other rail lines made it possible for the establishment of small suburbs. Riverside, Illinois, possibly the first suburban planned community, located just outside of Chicago, was designed by noted landscape architect Frederick Law Olmsted in 1869. The idea was of a quiet neighborhood, with space between you and your neighbor but with the convenience of urban amenities. Suburban life began to take root as the ideal way of life to achieve the American dream in late nineteenth-century America. This American dream, based on ideals of independence and upward mobility, was fully manifested in the phenomenon of suburbia. Kenneth T. Jackson's landmark book, *Crabgrass Frontier*, explains:

> *Suburbia symbolizes the fullest, most unadulterated embodiment of contemporary culture; it is a manifestation of such fundamental characteristics of American culture as conspicuous consumption, a reliance upon the private automobile, upward mobility, the separation of family into nuclear units, the widening division between work and leisure, and a tendency toward racial and economic exclusiveness.*[34]

The Great Depression and World War II interrupted that ideal, but the post–World War II period brought with it a housing shortage. The Federal Housing Administration intervened and introduced loan programs encouraging and facilitating the development of single-family, detached houses. But where would these houses be built? In 1956, President Dwight D. Eisenhower signed the Federal Aid Highway Act, which authorized $25 billion for the construction of forty-one thousand miles for an interstate highway system. Although actually intended for national defense, these highways made it possible for the houses to be built outside city limits while still being within a short drive from work. Cities began to stretch outward into previous rural areas as more and more young families settled into houses, achieving their version of the American dream. Some urban centers within cities actually lost population but grew physically anyway into the outlying countryside at the expense of their decaying inner cities. Whichever the case, new homes in 1950s suburbia were typically prefabricated, mass produced and inexpensive, facilitating the American dream.

As people made their homes and started families in these new suburbs, retail outlets soon followed. Downtown business districts were replaced by suburban all-in-one stores, fast-food restaurants, strip malls and shopping malls. The unplanned, uncontrolled spreading of urban development into areas adjoining the edge of a city—or "sprawl," as it was termed by the

Lexington sprawl. *Photo by author.*

*American Heritage Dictionary*—became the blueprint for virtually every city, of every region, in America.

Making all of this possible was the reliance of the American family on the automobile. Detroit pumped out millions of automobiles, which became more and more affordable to the American family. Where formerly there had been quiet two-lane country roads connecting distant towns together, these roads morphed into highways, strung intermittently with stoplights, to accommodate the traffic. Towns grew closer and closer together as suburbs stretched ever farther into the countryside. Traffic clogged the commercial-laden thoroughfares, and suburbia thrived. In the meantime, downtown business districts dried up, crumbled and were boarded up. The change in America's cultural and physical landscape, in a relatively short time, was dramatic, far-reaching and, ultimately, unsustainable.

In the 1990s, attitudes began to change as communities became stretched outward amidst the bottleneck traffic and congestion. Rising fuel costs, as well as questions of America's continued reliance on imported fossil fuel energy, caused many to pause and wonder if the current community model was sustainable for future generations. Opponents of sprawl further argued that because of the reliance on the automobile, even just to navigate from one store to another, communities became increasingly segregated, as the poor often were unable to afford an automobile. Without an automobile, and with public transportation in most cases erratic, inner-city residents did not have the same access to goods and services. Furthermore, low-density development into rural areas reduced the relative value of inner-city real estate. Sprawl was not only leaving its mark on the environment through increased emissions and pollution, but a social price was being paid as well.

Many were also alarmed that suburban sprawl threatened historic landmarks and landscapes. Civil War battlefields were and continue to be especially susceptible, especially in northern Virginia, currently one of the fastest-growing areas of the country. Manassas Battlefield fought to stave off sprawl from neighboring Washington, D.C., and achieved some level of success with its ability to fight off a proposed history theme park (along with a huge real estate development) by the Walt Disney Company. At Gettysburg, it is much the same: residential housing, fast-food restaurants and parking lots enclose, surround and threaten to undermine the integrity of the historic site. Currently, only 80 percent of the park's six thousand acres are under National Park Service protection.

At issue is a very simple question: what do we want our community to look like? Such a simple question leads to a multitude of different answers, and land development has become one of the most controversial issues of the day. Americans have different ideas about what they want their communities to look like. Issues of "growth as progress," individual liberty, the government's role in community development and homeowner property rights are issues where opinions greatly differ. There are two main issues of sprawl at stake: the environmental impact and the social impact.

The arguments over the environmental impact are fairly simple. Opponents of sprawl point out that suburban households use more natural resources, usually nonrenewable, to maintain their way of life. Families from suburbs drive 31 percent more than urban families, using more petroleum, rubber and other resources involved in transportation. More vehicle emissions are put into the air, and there is more noise and light pollution as well. Fragile ecosystems, containing numerous wildlife and plant life, are threatened or destroyed as cities encroach into the countryside. Water sources become contaminated, as pavement and concrete, unlike soil, do not provide a natural filtering process. Large suburban yards, heavily fertilized, run off into ditches, leading to contaminated streams. Centuries-old trees are cut down to make way for newer development.

The social impact of sprawl is just as devastating. Sprawl concentrates poverty to the inner city, which creates a culture of social problems—drug abuse, unemployment, violence and lack of opportunity—and increases inequality, while reducing social and economic mobility. Suburban life, while relying on automobile use, discourages or even makes walking impossible or dangerous. Most studies conclude that suburbanites not only tend to weigh more but also have a greater prevalence of hypertension than people from urban areas. Finally, suburban neighborhoods, with less density than urban ones, promote less of a sense of community, leading to isolationism.

Defenders of sprawl point out that the environmental argument, especially the traffic issue, is overblown. Better automobile design, regulation and cleaner fuel help alleviate much of the problem. "Sprawl," it is argued, "is simply the result of the free market at work, and cannot be limited without implementation of intrusive environmental government policies."[35]

And so it is in Kentucky as well, especially in the famed Inner Bluegrass Region. The two largest cities in Kentucky—Louisville and Lexington—both experienced tremendous growth after World War II. Lexington began to spill outward into the established thoroughbred farms in Fayette County. Later, the surrounding rural counties of Jessamine, Scott, Woodford and Bourbon began to feel Lexington push farther into its farmland, congesting their roads and threatening one of the very industries that made the region unique.

Losing even a small part of the thoroughbred industry would be disastrous to Kentucky, not only for the pride and the community identity that Kentuckians have in being the "horse capital of the world" (a title that has been the subject of lawsuits with another community in another state) but also for the economic benefits. These economic benefits are substantial. The economic impact of the entire equine industry in Kentucky is $4 billion. In a state that struggles with high unemployment rates, the equine industry generates between 80,000 and 100,000 jobs, both directly and indirectly.

The region has also attracted millions of tourists for over a century. The great horse Man o' War attracted thousands of adoring fans to his Faraway Farm outside of Lexington during the 1930s and 1940s. When the equine celebrity died in 1947, as many as two thousand people attended his funeral. Today, thousands of people come to the Inner Bluegrass Region to take in the incredible beauty of both the natural and cultural landscapes. Lexington is within one day's driving distance of 75 percent of the nation's population, making it an appealing destination.

The tourism options when visiting the region are varied and impressive. Shakertown, Henry Clay's estate (Ashland), the Mary Todd Lincoln House and several wineries and bourbon distilleries offer visitors a look and taste into Bluegrass culture. But for most, it is the equine-related attractions that draw visitors to this section of Kentucky. According to the Lexington Convention and Visitors' Bureau, over half (60 percent) of tourists come to the region to see horses. A visit to a working horse farm or the spacious grounds at the Kentucky Horse Park or watching training or racing at Keeneland gives visitors a feel for what makes the region truly special. Of the $8.8 billion economic impact of the state's tourism industry, the Bluegrass Region's equine industry is the number one promotional attraction. In 2009, the economic impact of tourism was a formidable $2.4 billion. This impact results in enormous benefits to the region because visitors translate into jobs. About 14,600 people are employed in equine tourism–related jobs in the Bluegrass Region.

These jobs, and the entire equine-themed culture of the region, have propelled Lexington into elite company as one of the top cities in America in a number of categories. In short, people would rather work, live and play in a community with an identity. The Lexington Chamber of Commerce compiled rankings from several sources, highlighting the attractiveness of the community. Lexington ranked in the top ten nationally in such categories as "Most Educated Workforce," "Best Mid-Sized Place to Start a New Business," "Best Place for Business and Careers," "Best Place for Relocating Families," "Quality of Life Metro" and "Best Cities for Education."

These attributes show that Lexington, and the Inner Bluegrass Region as a whole, are attractive to tourists and residents alike. With this comes a price. Despite provisions in place to curb unchecked growth, in the 1990s, Fayette County still lost just over 4,700 acres of farmland to development. A surge in growth from 1997 to 2002 resulted in another 19,508 agricultural acres lost to development, with the entire Inner Bluegrass Region losing 116 square miles.

The thoroughbred farms of the Bluegrass Region survived the Civil War armies marching through Kentucky, overcame anti-gambling reformers closing the markets for their products, but this new adversary would prove a formidable foe. In the following chapters, we will visit three historic thoroughbred farms—McGrathiana, Hamburg Place and Louisville's Bashford Manor—all in the way of growing communities. All three are lost, but the reader must decide if they were lost to sprawl or simply sacrificed for healthy communities to grow and prosper.

# 5

# MCGRATHIANA FARM

The old McGrathiana Farm sits on the north side of Lexington along the busy Newtown Pike, a bustling four-lane road that is one of the main corridors from Interstates 64 and 75 into downtown Lexington. The front entrance to the once-proud estate—two stone columns holding a centuries' old gate—stands stoically, looking out of place along the busy highway, now lined with hotels, gas stations and office buildings. When McGrathiana was established in the early 1870s, it was rural countryside, located about three miles from a burgeoning Lexington.

The founder of McGrathiana was the roguish Henry Price McGrath, a native Kentuckian born in 1814 in the tiny hamlet of Keene, in Woodford County, in the heart of the Bluegrass Region. McGrath was a pious young boy who grew up in poverty and loved to sing in the local country church. Later in life, McGrath liked to the relay the story that he was denied a formal education over two cents: "He gave the first dime he ever made in his life to a wealthy neighbor, requesting the latter to bring with him back the blue-back speller from the city. The neighbor came back empty-handed with the comment 'The book cost 12 cents.'"[36] McGrath was soon to be educated in other things.

As a teenager, McGrath was trained as a tailor and toiled in that trade until he moved to nearby Lexington at the age of twenty-one and discovered he could make more money assisting crooked dice games during the horse-racing meets. He found his calling, and he was determined to be good at it. The formerly straitlaced country boy began to develop a more robust and worldly personality. According to one acquaintance, he was "a hearty eater and could hold his liquor, sing the gay and ribald songs of the day, bend boys back with laughter over a dirty joke, and also speak with authority on horses."[37]

After a short time down the Mississippi River in Vicksburg, Mississippi, possibly working as a tailor, McGrath was beckoned west to California in the gold rush of 1849, but not to panhandle for gold. He used his Lexington racetrack education and did what he knew best—take the money at the crooked gambling tables of unsuspecting and largely

H.P. McGrath, a rogue, gambler and winner of the first Kentucky Derby. *Courtesy of the Kentucky Derby Museum.*

uneducated gold diggers. In doing so, he made a small fortune. Restless and looking for new opportunities (or possibly run out of the area), McGrath left California sometime in the mid-1850s.

His next stop was the great racing town of New Orleans, which flourished during the winter months, as every year midwestern stables quartered their horses in the warmer climate. McGrath partnered with two other gamblers, James Sherwood and Henry Perritt, to create one of the first swanky and elegant gambling houses in that city, catering to the tastes of wealthy merchants, planters and horseman of the Crescent City, as well as the population, which swelled during the winter. Sherwood, a North Carolinian, was described as easygoing and witty, a self-made gentleman who had worked his way up from humble beginnings. Sherwood was known as a great storyteller and enjoyed spinning yarns to the merriment of his patrons—all while taking their money at the gambling tables.

McGrath and Sherwood, along with Henry Perritt, spent nearly $70,000 to renovate the famed Boston Club. Their gambling house became known for its sumptuous dinners and comfortable card rooms, as well as the place to gamble on thoroughbreds throughout the winter months. It was known as the headquarters for all southern and western turfmen who made New Orleans their home throughout the winter as they campaigned their horses at the nearby racetracks. McGrath and Company, as the club became known, prospered greatly in the days just before the Civil War, with McGrath as host, entertaining with his flashy dress and signature red necktie.

The Boston Club closed with the advent of the Civil War in 1861. Both Sherwood and Perritt threw their energies and wealth toward the Confederate cause. Sherwood gave large sums of money, clothing and equipment for troops stationed in New Orleans, while Perritt organized and equipped a company of soldiers called the Perritt Guards, sent to his native state of Virginia to fight the Yankees.

McGrath tried to stay out of the conflict but ran into problems with Union general Benjamin Butler, the military governor of New Orleans, and headed back home to Kentucky for a short-lived visit until things cooled off in New Orleans. Butler was reassigned in 1863, and McGrath traveled back down the Mississippi to New Orleans to reopen his famed gambling house. Unfortunately for him, he ran afoul again of the Federal authorities for scamming the Northern soldiers with allegedly fixed horse races. He was sentenced to a year in jail, which he served as his finances on the outside dried up.

After his release in 1864, he landed in St. Louis to reignite his "business career" and partnered with Johnny Chamberlin, a disreputable gambling house owner. Chamberlin, a small-time player with big ambitions, dreamed of establishing a large-scale gambling operation in New York City. With McGrath's connections and experience, the two set out for New York City to strike it big. They arrived in the Big Apple during the cold winter of 1864.

McGrath and Chamberlin needed more capital to establish a first-class gambling house, or "skinning house," as they were sometimes called. They got their break when former bare-knuckle boxer and future Tammany Hall–backed congressman John Morrissey included the two in a syndicate to establish a swanky gambling house on Fifth Avenue in Manhattan. Morrissey had impressive connections, entertaining such notables as former presidents Chester Arthur, Rutherford B. Hayes and Ulysses S. Grant at his posh gambling house at Saratoga Springs, located at the racetrack he helped found. McGrath's main job in the organization was to use his "marketing skills" to lure unsuspecting out-of-towners into the gambling house. With its elegant staircases, crystal chandeliers and excellent food, the company was an instant success. Many of the patrons were contractors, government officials and stock brokers all speculating, and in many instances making millions, on the Civil War economy. McGrath and his associates were eager to relieve many of them of much of their newfound wealth. Within the first four months of operation, McGrath had become a rich man again.

Evidently, internal disagreements abounded within the partnership, and McGrath and Chamberlin left the syndicate. Chamberlin opened another posh gambling house in the city, which he ran for years in competition with Morrisey. In 1870, he opened a thoroughbred racetrack and clubhouse called Monmouth Park in the resort town of Long Branch in New Jersey. Chamberlin also later had the distinction of owning the thoroughbred racehorse Survivor, winner of the first Preakness Stakes in 1873.

McGrath took his profits, which ranged from $200,000 to $1,000,000, and went back home to Kentucky. He was also determined to get into the horse-racing business—but instead of operating a track, he desired to be a country gentleman horse breeder, especially of thoroughbred racehorses.

McGrathiana mansion, patterned after the U.S. Hotel in Saratoga, New York. *Courtesy of the Kentucky Derby Museum.*

He bought a 416-acre farm, known as the old Gilbert farm, and built a grand mansion, patterned after the U.S. Hotel at Saratoga Springs, which he named McGrathiana. He was a fifty-three-year-old bachelor and was ready to make his mark on thoroughbred racing.

The Victorian era approached with its extremely stiff, cold and uncompromising rules of how to conduct oneself in upper-class society. Although McGrath had the money to command a certain amount of respect among the upper classes of Lexington, H.P. McGrath would never completely fit in with that society with his boisterous and freewheeling ways. His habit of wearing bright red neckties was considered flashy and inappropriate by many of his conservative Bluegrass neighbors. They probably were not pleased to have a former racketeer, hustler and prisoner as their new neighbor. With time, however, he would be accepted by most in the region because of his hospitality and gregarious nature. The parties, or "burgoos," as they were called, thrown at McGrathiana were not to be missed—although many would probably not admit it at the time.

Despite his neighbors' raised eyebrows, McGrath began assembling an impressive roster of thoroughbred stallions and broodmares. McGrath also hired expert horsemen, most of them African American, to work with training, handling and grooming the horses. His head trainer was Ansel Williamson, who had worked at R.A. Alexander's Woodburn Farm, becoming known as one of the eminent horsemen of the time. McGrath hired Williamson, and soon they were winning races, not just in the "western" region, as it was called, but also at the elite eastern tracks run by his former cohorts.

The first horse to achieve prominence from McGrathiana was a son of the great Woodburn Farm stallion Lexington, named Tom Bowling. The horse had a reputation of being vicious, although McGrath claimed he was "as sweet tempered as a horse could be."[38] Despite this claim, McGrath, with a wink, mentioned that he "generally kept an empty feed bag over his nose to keep the horse from hurting anyone."[39] McGrath also claimed that Tom Bowling was the greatest horse he ever owned, and his record substantiates that claim: In seventeen starts, he was a winner fourteen times, including at the 1873 Travers Stakes, probably at that time the most prestigious race in the East. At Saratoga Race Course, in front of his old crony and now rival, John Morrissey, Tom Bowling beat the best horses of the East.

McGrath's playful personality shines in a newspaper account of the day leading up to the premier race for three-year-olds at the time:

*While the horse munched his oats, McGrath fondled the brute and got into conversation with him: Now, Tom, are you going to behave yourself and win the Travers Stakes for me?...He winks his eye at me, which is his way of saying I'm all right, go out and bet.*

After taking the winner's cup from Mr. William Travers at the presentation stand, a jubilant McGrath said to the crowd, "I will keep this cup filled with fine wines tonight in town. Come and see if you can drink it until it is empty."[40]

For the 1875 racing season, McGrath's stable was loaded with talent, with the headliners being Calvin, Chesapeake and Aristides, all three-year-old colts. Calvin was a half brother to Tom Bowling, both the sons of dam Lucy Fowler. Chesapeake, another son of the great Lexington, was considered by McGrath to be the star of the barn. McGrath sent Chesapeake and Aristides to Louisville to run at the Louisville Jockey Club's new racetrack, to contend for their feature race, the Kentucky Derby.

Of the fifteen starters in the inaugural Kentucky Derby, Chesapeake was considered the class of the field. Chesapeake's running style was a closer; he preferred to let others set the pace, biding his time before making a big run at the end. To ensure a quick pace up front, McGrath entered Aristides as a "rabbit" to soften up the other frontrunners, allowing Chesapeake to pick up the pieces and win. Aristides was not intended to win. The well-bred chestnut colt by Leamington, and out of the Lexington mare Sarong, had the deck stacked against him even more due to a race in Lexington about a week before. Trying to maneuver around a heavy, muddy track drenched by recent rains, he became unbalanced, cutting his legs with his horseshoes as he ran.

He didn't have to worry about mud a week later. The first Derby Day in Louisville came up bright and sunny, and although it was a Monday afternoon, a crowd of about ten thousand packed the brand-new Louisville Jockey Club Racetrack. The Kentucky Derby, the second race of the day, to be run in midafternoon, featured a lucrative purse, with $2,850 going to the winner. Most gamblers believed Chesapeake had the best chance to take first prize.

But Chesapeake never had a chance. After a slow start, the horse never found his rhythm and lingered far back in the pack, never challenging. Aristides, under the guidance of nineteen-year-old African American jockey Oliver Lewis, broke smartly away from the starting line and settled in amongst the front-runners. When the horses reached the homestretch, Aristides held a short lead but was setting a blistering pace. "Where's Chesapeake?" jockey Lewis thought as he wondered how long Aristides could hold out. McGrath, stationed at the head of the stretch, yelled at Lewis to "Keep on! Keep on!" Lewis and Aristides kept on and held off late charges from Volcano and Verdigris to win the race by two lengths. The time for the mile and a half was 2:37.75, the fastest recording at that distance for three-year-olds. Not bad for the second stringer.

Aristides continued to impress as McGrath took his stable east to compete against the top competition in the country. Aristides also won the prestigious Withers and Jerome Stakes, both times beating the best the East had to offer, as well as his own stablemate Chesapeake. He most certainly would have also won the ninth running of the Belmont Stakes if not for the shenanigans of McGrath. Once again, the plan was for Aristides to be the rabbit to set up the victory for his stablemates—this time both Calvin and Chesapeake.

Ever the gambler and ready to make a killing, McGrath bet heavily on Calvin and was determined to skew the results if need be. What transpired was an obvious fix of the race. Aristides, off slow, made a tremendous move in the latter stages of the race, passing horse after horse, with only his stablemate Calvin left to pass. As he began to overtake the tiring Calvin, Jockey Lewis pulled hard on the reins, prompting the incensed crowd to yell, "Turn loose that horse!" Calvin crossed the finish line first, and McGrath walked away with $30,000 in winning bets.

Aristides finished his racing career three years later in 1878, a winner of nine out of twenty-one starts. He was retired to stud at McGrathiana, where his prospects were in demand, given his exceptional pedigree. In 1987, a bronze statue of the horse was erected at Churchill Downs, the site of his greatest victory.

McGrathiana, by this time, was not only known for its fast horses but also for the lavish parties that McGrath hosted on the grounds. Each spring and fall, on the Sunday before the opening of the Lexington race meets, McGrath opened the doors of his mansion and grounds, serving as much burgoo and bourbon as one could consume. May McKinney Neal wrote about her memories of a McGrathiana party that took place in 1872:

> We children helped gather the wild ferns for the table, the cress for the salad and the mint for the sauce. We watched with awe the whole South Down lambs that were being turned eternally on their spits above the fire of hickory wood. We danced around the great caldron of burgoo as they threw in whole chickens, whole squirrels, bushels of tomatoes, green peppers, okra, tarragon, more peppers—while round and round the old cook stirred the brew for hours and hours.[41]

Statue of the first Derby winner, Aristides, in the Churchill Downs garden paddock. *Photo by author.*

Aristides, Calvin and Chesapeake would have all been yearlings, tromping around the fields with their mothers.

Always ready to show off his prize horseflesh, it was common for McGrath to parade his horses in front of the admiring guests, telling stories—or bragging—about their impressive victories on the track. At the feast in 1872, McKinney Neal remembered that McGrath even liked to show off his neighbor's horses:

> *Uncle Price* [McGrath] *arose—handsome, gray-eyed and close bearded…he said "My friends, one moment. We have a surprise for you. Will you all turn to the West?" Then around the corner of the house came a little stable boy leading a tall, shining bay horse—proud but gentle, he moved like music, and no one spoke until he stopped in the middle of the lawn. "Gentleman," it was Price McGrath speaking again, "Our neighbor Harper has loaned us his treasure for our pleasure. This is Longfellow! Hats off in the presence of a King!"* [42]

The seventeen-hand Longfellow was owned by John Harper of Nantura Stud and had just recently retired, winning fourteen of sixteen races. From the reception he got from McGrath's party guests, he also was quite a celebrity.

The years of eating and drinking massive quantities took their toll on McGrath's health, but McGrath still maintained a hectic travel schedule, campaigning his horses heavily in Kentucky in the spring and then to the tracks on the East Coast, still run mainly by his old business partners. He nearly won the third running of the Kentucky Derby. His colt Leonard led all the way around the track until it was passed and beaten by Baden-Baden. His horse Wissahickon finished last of nine in the 1879 running of the Derby. The 1881 Derby was his last shot; he entered two colts, although neither would contend.

Just two months after that Derby, Hal Price McGrath was dead of a diseased liver and dropsy. He died on July 5, 1881, at his old friend and fellow racketeer Johnny Chamberlin's Central Hotel in Long Branch, New Jersey. His obituary mentioned what he was most known for in the Bluegrass Region: "His hospitality was unbounded…every turfman was invited to make himself at home."[43]

A dispersal sale was held to sell McGrath's thoroughbred stock, which at this time contained forty-one horses. Aristides, at this time an unproven sire, was sold to Albert Hankins of Chicago for $3,400. Aristides stood at Hankins's stud farm in Hebron, Indiana, for several years and, after proving to be a disappointment at stud, switched hands several more times before his death in obscurity in St. Louis in 1893. He was buried there in an unmarked grave.

One year after the thoroughbred stock was dispersed, the mansion and grounds were auctioned for $46,912.50 to Lexington native Colonel Milton Young. Young was no doubt a frequent visitor to the feasts held by McGrath, and as a tribute to the former owner, he decided to keep the farm's name, McGrathiana. Young, who had made a fortune in both tobacco and hardware, was deeply involved in racing in Kentucky and was a founding member of the Kentucky Racing Commission. Described as "shrewd, self reliant, ambitious, and thoroughly in love with his business,"[44] Colonel Young kept the McGrathiana reputation and product strong with an impressive roster of stallions, such as Duke of Montrose, Onondaga, Strathmore, Longstreet and Potomac.

Young's greatest stallion was Hanover, a champion racer for the Dwyer brothers. In his first two years of racing, Hanover won an astounding twenty-seven of thirty starts, and upon retirement in 1889, he was the richest money winner for that time. For all of his on-track accolades, he may have even been better in the breeding shed. Hanover topped the United States sire list four consecutive years, from 1895 to 1898, with his best being Hamburg, the American Horse of the Year in 1898. Hanover died prematurely in 1899, just as he was coming into his prime as a truly great sire.

It was during this time that the reform movement began to have devastating effects on the thoroughbred industry. Adverse turf regulations, at both the state and national levels, caused many racetracks to go out of business. Thoroughbred farms all over the Bluegrass struggled because of a sharp drop in the demand for thoroughbreds. Longtime Bluegrass icon and Freeland Stock Farm owner Ed Corrigan created a sensation when he announced that he was leaving the thoroughbred business after many decades. Colonel Young, a mainstay in thoroughbred racing for many decades, followed suit and announced in July 1908, that he, too, was leaving the thoroughbred business, "unless there is relief by November."[45] The climate did not change, and just a month later, McGrathiana, and all of its bloodstock, was put up for sale. According to a newspaper article that October, Young planned to start a breeding farm in the Argentine Republic. This plan did not materialize, and by October of that year, he was quoted as saying he was "sorry to leave the business."[46]

The new owners were cattle breeders R.A. and W.S. Beasley of Lancaster, Kentucky. The Beasley brothers only owned the farm for seven years before the farm was sold once again, this time to Charles B. Shaffer of Chicago, and turned back into a thoroughbred breeding farm. Shaffer, who made a fortune from oil wells in Pennsylvania, bred both thoroughbreds and standardbreds on the farm. He also made many physical changes to the farm, the most striking in 1928, when he tore down the original Neoclassical-style mansion that H.P. McGrath had built and replaced it with an even larger Craftsman-style mansion, now called the Carnahan House. Shaffer also changed the name of the property to Coldstream Farm, the name the property still uses. Shaffer struck gold when he bought a thoroughbred English stallion named Bull Dog for $80,000, once again maintaining the property as a premier breeding operation. Bull Dog sired fifty-two stakes winners, including Bull Lea, which would go on to become Calumet Farm's foundation sire a generation later.

After Shaffer's death in 1943, the McGrathiana property began to be subdivided, first by Interstate 75, which split the property into two parcels. Unlike neighboring farms, which were being swallowed by a developing Newtown Pike corridor, with typical types of businesses associated with sprawl—gas stations, restaurants and hotels—McGrathiana would undergo a different kind of development.

Ultra-wealthy cosmetics tycoon Elizabeth Arden purchased the 722-acre northern section of the farm and named it Maine Chance Farm. Arden owned one of the top racing stables in the 1940s and 1950s, winning the 1947 Kentucky Derby with Jet Pilot. Arden died in 1966, and the property was sold to the University of Kentucky, which had already bought the southern portion of the Coldstream property ten years earlier.

Standardbred breeder Henry Knight, of Almahurst Farm fame, bought the southern part of McGrathiana (Coldstream) for about $2,000,000 and mainly raised standardbreds. In 1956, Knight sold this portion of the farm, about 750 acres of farmland, barns and the Craftsman-style mansion that Shaffer had built, to the University of Kentucky (UK) for $1,123,500. The university, also eventually purchasing several other farms in the area, intended to use the property as an agricultural experiment station as part of its Department of Animal Sciences for its College of Agriculture. For about seven years, the university used the Craftsman-style mansion that Charles Shaffer built on the property as an alumni center, hosting parties, dinners and conferences. The house was called the Carnahan House, after a prominent alumnus and benefactor who paid for much of the remodeling.

The university has owned the land as long as anyone, and the story of the land's development, and lack thereof, is full of many twists and turns, misguided intentions, lawsuits and controversy. The land became very valuable, mainly because it sat between Interstate 64 and downtown Lexington along the busy Newtown Pike.

The university used much of the property as an extension of the classroom, researching equine and agricultural-related issues. The university continues to maintain a strong presence at the campus, branching out to include non-equine-related research and technologies: the UK Veterinary and Diagnostic Laboratory, a UK-affiliated, technology-based businesses; pharmaceutical manufacturer Coldstream Laboratories, Inc.; and the Center for Applied Energy Research.

The focus of the university changed at Coldstream in the 1990s, from not-for-profit to for-profit enterprises. An example of this is tenant Coldstream Enterprises. "Initially we were an academic unit at UK focused on new drug formulation and manufacturing," explained CEO Dr. Joseph Wyse in 2008. "We have undergone a massive paradigm shift. We are [now] a stand-alone company, a for-profit venture."[47] Besides the shift in focus for many

Coldstream tenants, the lure to sell parcels of this valuable land has proven difficult for the university to resist over the years.

In 1987, facing budget shortfalls, the university began a study of potential ways to profit off the valuable piece of property. The next year, university vice-chancellor for administration Jack C. Blanton said that Coldstream "was at the top of the pack of valuable land to be developed"[48] and that "developers are salivating over the prospect." By 1989, the university, "in serious need of additional revenue," gave consideration to selling part of McGrathiana to be developed as a ninety-five-acre retail shopping mall. Board of trustees member Lawrence E. Forgy Jr. implored the board to "consider carefully whether the board has any option in view of the financial condition of the institution." He estimated that between $50 and $70 million could be made "over the full life of a lease" in the project.[49]

The university ultimately rejected developing the mall, instead focusing on developing the land as a research park. After fits and starts, development began to hit its stride in 1991 with the advent of knowledge-based firms. Since then, other businesses have located to the campus, including a 300,000-square-foot, 239-bed hospital, scheduled to be completed in 2012. This would push the employee population at Coldstream to well over two thousand people.

With the pressures of attracting new tenants, a research firm was hired in 2008 to study how the campus could "redesign itself in a way that better fits the lifestyles of the growing number of professionals setting up shop there."[50] That meant the inclusion of service-based amenities—restaurants, delivery companies, day-care centers, fitness gyms and other businesses—to meet the needs of the growing professional population. Would the cultural landscape of the old McGrathiana now also include these types of businesses?

Coldstream Research campus is currently under development by research-based companies, with the potential for service-based businesses to follow. Some would say this development is inappropriate, given the historic nature of the property. What cannot be argued is that the social, professional and economic impact of companies to which the campus is home greatly benefits the area. Many of the businesses at Coldstream contribute greatly to society as a whole; breakthroughs in biochemistry, pharmaceuticals, equine health and psychiatric health have taken place at the research campus. Furthermore, these are companies projected to be in the area for a very long time, increasing the tax base and the quality of life of the area. These are the types of jobs that prompted *Forbes* magazine to name Lexington as the fifth best city in the United States for "Business and Careers" and the fifth best city in the nation for young professionals. Another positive feature of the property, ensuring a "green character" for that area, was the construction of a 1.8-mile section of the Legacy Trail, a 12.0-mile walking, biking and interpretive trail.

Lexington surely lost an important piece of its history with the development of McGrathiana. The property unfortunately faced several major obstacles to remaining a thoroughbred farm. First, it was located too close to growing Lexington. Even by nineteenth-century standards, McGrath's farm was not as rural as were many of his neighbors' farms. Second, and along the same reasoning as the previous point, the farm was located within Lexington's Urban Services Boundary, making the property eligible for development. Third, it was located on a major thoroughfare; Newtown Pike connects Lexington with Interstates 64 and 75, making the land very valuable. Fourth, the type of development at the old McGrathiana is the type of development that every community needs in order to be vibrant, relevant and contributing to the greater good of its citizens.

H.P. McGrath would not feel at home today at McGrathiana. His grand mansion, barns, outbuildings, livestock and beloved horses are long gone.

Equine tombstones on the Coldstream Research campus. *Photo by author.*

# McGrathiana Farm

Today's view from McGrathiana. *Photo by author.*

Coldstream Research campus, formerly McGrathiana Farm. *Photo by author.*

The parties he threw, with their endless supply of burgoo, champagne and embellished stories of victories and defeats on racetracks from New York to Kentucky, are but echoes on the landscape. He would also probably not feel at home among the professionals who make up the current McGrathiana population. That is, of course, unless he could swindle a few out of some hard-earned money in a crooked dice game in a parking lot behind a pharmaceutical company.

# 6

# HAMBURG PLACE

W hen you type in the words "Hamburg Place, Lexington, Kentucky" on an Internet search engine, the first page or so will list what Hamburg Place is today—an area filled with an array of shopping opportunities. Bookstores, department stores, office supply stores, shoe stores, restaurants, theaters and portrait studios are choices offered to shoppers. Several hotels dot the property, as does an office park containing a variety of smaller businesses: a store specializing in olive oils, a jeweler advertising interest in buying gold, a store dedicated to Halloween costumes and several doctors' offices. There is even a small business college.

Not only can one shop at Hamburg Place, but one can live there as well. Residential developments, consisting of single-family town homes and condominiums, are also part of the current Hamburg Place landscape. Included in this area are a swimming pool and a cabana recreation area. In short, just about anything you want to do or buy, you can do at Hamburg Place; it has "every conceivable amenity,"[51] as one advertisement proclaims. But you won't see many horses.

You will, however, see allusions to its namesake's former glory. Names such as Old Rosebud, Sir Barton, Plaudit, Alysheba, Pink Pigeon, Star Shoot, Paul Jones and Grey Lag are now either street or office complex names in and around today's version of Hamburg Place. Today, many shoppers and visitors probably wonder where these interesting, and sometimes bizarre, names come from. These were the names of horses that, a century ago, made Hamburg Place one of the greatest thoroughbred breeding operations in the world.

The list of Hamburg Place accomplishments in racing is jarring. From 1918 to 1927, ten consecutive years, Hamburg Place was the leading breeding farm in America. Fourteen thoroughbred champions were bred here. Five Kentucky Derby winners and five Belmont Stakes winners, including Sir Barton, the first American Triple Crown winner, came from Hamburg Place. It was the farm where John Madden, founder of Hamburg Place, became known in racing circles as the "Master of the Turf."

John Edward Madden was born in Bethlehem, Pennsylvania, in 1856 to Irish immigrants Patrick and Catherine Madden. His father died when John was only three years old, leaving behind his widow and three children—a four-year-old daughter, John and a seven-month-old son. Virtually every account of Madden's early life focuses attention on his athleticism. Nearly six feet tall and solidly built, Madden took pride in his athletic exploits, an aspect of his personality that lasted his entire life. As a teenager, he excelled at baseball, running, broad jumping and boxing. He exercised daily as an adult and built his own gymnasium on the grounds of Hamburg Place. Madden's biographer, Kent Hollingsworth, relayed that at the age of sixty, Madden swam the thirty-yard length of his spring-fed pond every day, rain or shine, no matter the season. He did not smoke and only rarely drank alcohol.[52]

As a teenager in Pennsylvania, Madden developed an interest in trotting horses, at first racing them himself at the local county fairs and then buying, selling and trading them. It wasn't long before this ambitious and energetic young man began to make his mark in the standardbred market. Even at such a young age, he took business risks that usually ended with him pocketing a nice profit. One such risk occurred in 1889, when Madden traveled to England and bought a standardbred named Warlock, a stallion with a desired pedigree cross, at a low price. Upon returning to America, Madden stood Warlock for stud for six months before selling the stallion for $15,000. In another deal, he spent $1,500 for a mare named Geneva S., only to resell her shortly after for $15,000. Madden continued climbing the ranks in the trotting business, but the thoroughbred market, a more lucrative business, beckoned. In 1891, a thirty-five-year-old Madden packed his bags and moved to Lexington to try his hand at thoroughbreds. At a time when many people were leaving the industry due to Progressive-era reforms, Madden was just getting in.

In Lexington, Madden continued training, owning and dealing standardbred horses, but over time, his focus changed from standardbreds to thoroughbreds. The breed may have changed, but his success did not. In typical Madden fashion, in 1888 he bought the colt Castaway II for $1,500 and just ten days later resold him for a $100 profit. Castaway II went on to have an excellent racing career, winning the Brooklyn Handicap for the Beverwyck Stable in 1890.

In 1896, after several more years of success in the thoroughbred industry, Madden bought a horse named Hamburg for $1,600 (some sources give the price at $1,200) from Lexington-based Elmendorf Farm. Hamburg was sired by the great Hanover, a precocious horse that won his first seventeen starts and the leading American stallion at the time. Hamburg took after his father in two ways: one, he was very fast; and two, he was very headstrong. Although Madden claimed that Hamburg was the most difficult horse he ever trained, he turned in a spectacular two-year-old season, winning twelve of sixteen starts and never placing out of the money, despite consistently carrying high weights.

Hamburg wasn't the only exceptional horse in the stable. In September 1896, Madden bought a two-year-old colt named Plaudit, which won several stakes races in October. Plaudit, although not the equal of Hamburg, won the Kentucky Derby by a nose the following year and then won the prestigious Clark Stakes at Churchill Downs. Madden was listed as both the owner and trainer of Plaudit, giving Madden the distinction as the only person ever to train, own and breed a Kentucky Derby winner. Madden sold Plaudit in New York later that year to W.C. Whitney for $25,000, only to buy him back later in the year for $12,000.

In December 1898, as Hamburg finished his splendid two-year-old campaign, Madden sold the colt for a record-breaking $40,001 to wealthy copper magnate Marcus Daly. (The previous record price for a horse in training was $40,000, thus the extra dollar was added to break the record.) Hamburg only raced five times as a three-year-old, and won four, before being retired to stud. Madden used the earnings from the sale of Hamburg to purchase a 235-acre farm located on the Winchester Pike, just outside Lexington. Originally called Overton Place, Madden changed the name to Hamburg Place, in honor of the horse that made Madden a household name in the thoroughbred business.

By this time, Madden had married the former Marie Anna Louise Megrue of Cincinnati. Two sons were born to the couple, J. Edward Jr. in 1894 and Joseph McKee in 1899. Their marriage, however, proved to be short-lived. One of the reasons Marie Anna cited in the divorce proceedings in 1906 was her "tiredness of living on a thoroughbred farm." Years of legal proceedings

# Hamburg Place

Hamburg Place, birthplace of five Kentucky Derby winners. *Courtesy of the Lexington History Museum.*

followed, made more complicated by Madden taking the children out of a convent and whisking them off to Hamburg Place after his wife made clear her desire to permanently take the children to Europe. Before the divorce was finalized, Marie Anna further complicated proceedings by marrying a wealthy New York broker, Louis Valentine Bell, although she could not divorce herself from thoroughbred racing. Bell was listed as a turfman as well. Madden eventually divorced Marie Anna officially in 1909, after gaining permanent custody of his two sons. He never remarried.

Hamburg Place grew as Madden continued juggling his training, owning, breeding and selling responsibilities. Eventually, the farm swelled to about two thousand acres as Madden purchased adjoining properties. The main residence, while not as elegant or gaudy as some of the Victorian-era mansions at other farms, stood solidly up a short lane and reflected the pragmatic nature of training and raising horses. Madden seemed more concerned about the comfort of his horses than he was for himself. He built two large training barns, both with exceptionally large shed rows, allowing two horses to jog side by side as they would on a track during inclement weather. An avid outdoorsman himself, he believed that horses were happier and healthier if they spent more time outside and less time in the barn. He designed a three-sided shed, or "run-in" shed, so his young horses could enter and exit at any time, giving the horses more freedom. Fencing was painted a utilitarian black rather than the more fashionable and visually striking white that adorned most other Bluegrass farms.

Hamburg Place, in its heyday, became a small city with a population of three hundred people working on the property. Nine family cottages and two large dormitories housed Madden's workers. Fifteen of those workers were exercise boys, who worked out the horses on a five-and-a-half-furlong training track. Tutors were provided, and the boys were sent to church every Sunday. Working for Madden was rewarding, but discipline was held in the highest regard. There was to be no profanity or noisy conduct, and visitors were to be treated courteously at all times. Another Madden rule: "No complaint received unless accompanied by a remedy."[53]

In 1912, Madden officially gave up training to focus on the owning, breeding and especially selling of horses. His training accomplishments were impressive. In just twenty-four years, he conditioned eight thoroughbred champions, including King James, sired by his Derby winner Plaudit and considered the Champion Handicap Male of 1909. Madden was listed as the nation's leading trainer from 1901 to 1903. He published an article for the *New York Herald* entitled "Modern Training Methods" in 1910, explaining many of his theories on training horses.

He began by writing about what he knew best about both human and equine athletes, extolling the virtues of a sound diet and exercise. "First and foremost, I would say regular feeding, good oats and hay, bran and grass, and regular work"[54] were essential to the success of the horse. In the following paragraphs, he gave learned opinions on topics such as breeding for speed and stamina, the importance of having a good staff working with the horse and the present thoroughbred breed (as it was in the early twentieth century) compared to their ancestors. The article was littered with homespun quotes; for example, regarding a thoroughbred's size equating to success on the racetrack, he said, "Many big turnips are hollow."[55] Madden's dry sense of humor came through as well, with such astute observations as "It is easy to train a good horse" and "Don't overlook the necessity of having an owner with plenty of money."[56]

During the time when the Progressive-era reformers threatened to destroy thoroughbred racing, many notable breeders dispersed their stock. Madden, on the other hand, believed it was a perfect time to buy. It was in 1912 that

Sir Barton, the first Triple Crown winner. *Courtesy of Churchill Downs Inc., Kinetic Corporation.*

Madden bought his most successful stallion, the European import Star Shoot. Star Shoot was America's leading stallion in 1911 and continued his success for Madden in 1912, producing ten stakes winners. Later, he sired the first Triple Crown winner, Sir Barton, which raced four times unsuccessfully for Madden as a two-year-old and then was sold to Canadian J.K.L. Ross, who purchased the colt for $10,000. Madden never regretted selling the horse, always saying it was better to sell too early than too late.

Just two years later, Star Shoot produced another champion, Grey Lag. Sold for another $10,000 as a yearling to Max Hirsch, who later sold the colt for $60,000 to Harry Sinclair, Grey Lag took the East Coast racetracks by storm and was named Horse of the Year for 1921. Later, Madden would call Grey Lag the greatest horse he ever bred.

Other great thoroughbreds bred at Hamburg Place were Old Rosebud, from the 1911 crop, which would win the Kentucky Derby in 1914 in track-record time; the unspectacular but steady 1920 Derby winner Paul Jones, which had the unfortunate problem of being a three-year-old the same year as Man o' War; 1923 Derby winner Zev, which, upon retirement in 1924, was the richest money earner in thoroughbred history; and Flying Ebony, which relished the mud and won the 1925 Derby in mud several inches deep. Belmont winners included Joe Madden (1909), named after his son, and the Finn (1915).

The best thoroughbred filly bred at Hamburg Place was Princess Doreen, sired by Spanish Prince, an imported stallion known for producing sprinters. Princess Doreen raced ninety-four times and won thirty-four, earning over $174,000—the highest-earning race mare of her time. She beat the boys regularly during her career, including a two-time Horse of the Year, Sarazan, in the Saratoga Handicap.

Although most attention is given to Madden's thoroughbred champions, he continued to breed standardbred horses on a smaller scale with much success and was elected posthumously to the Standardbred Hall of Fame in 1959. Horses of note were Hamburg Belle, which, after establishing a two-heat time record, sold for $40,000 in 1909. Hamburg Belle died later in the year, and the usually unsentimental Madden paid the shipping costs to have her brought back to Hamburg. She was the first horse buried in Madden's equine cemetery. Later, in a bit of wishful thinking, Madden believed this cemetery would rival Mammoth Cave and Henry Clay's estate as top Kentucky tourist attractions.

In 1929, at the age of seventy-two, the ever-vigorous and health-conscious Madden contracted pneumonia in New York City. Madden himself did not believe it to be anything serious, but on November 3, he had a heart attack and died alone in his hotel room. His body was brought to Lexington and buried at Calvary Cemetery. He left behind a fortune, estimated at $2 million.

His two sons, while growing up surrounded by horses, were not interested in continuing the thoroughbred legacy at Hamburg Place. The younger son, Joseph Madden, sold his share of the property to his older brother, John Edward Jr., who moved with his wife and two children from Tulsa to live at Hamburg Place, keeping the property in the Madden family. A Princeton graduate (both brothers graduated from Princeton) and polo enthusiast, John Edward Madden was a successful businessman and president of the Hubbinger Company, an Iowa-based manufacturer of corn products.

The thoroughbred part of our story at Hamburg Place did not end with John Madden's death in 1929. Grandsons Patrick and Preston eventually inherited the farm after their father's tragic suicide in 1943. Both lived on the property. Patrick, a lawyer, settled into the farmhouse, while Preston and his wife, Anita, lived in one of the dormitories his grandfather had built. It was

Preston who resurrected Hamburg Place back into a leading thoroughbred farm. Not only did he begin to bring top stallions back to the farm, but he also brought in an equine celebrity. In 1958, he bought the legendary Triple Crown winner War Admiral, at this time twenty-four years old, to live the remaining years of his life comfortably on the farm.

Preston Madden purchased California Derby winner T.V. Lark in 1960, after the horse's owner died. T.V. Lark, primarily a turf horse, won several important stakes races as a three-year-old. As a four-year-old, his biggest win came in the Washington, D.C. International, setting a track record and beating the renowned Kelso. He was named the Eclipse Award winner for Outstanding Male Turf Horse for 1961. At stud, T.V. Lark was a success, topping the United States sire earnings in 1974. The next year, T.V. Lark died at the age of eighteen and was buried at the farm cemetery.

Then, in 1984, possibly the greatest thoroughbred ever bred at Hamburg Place was born. His name was Alysheba. The promising son of Alydar sold as a yearling for $500,000 to Dorothy and Pam Scharbauer and was put under the care of trainer Jack van Berg to begin his racing career. Despite tripping and nearly falling running down the Churchill Downs homestretch, Alysheba recovered to win by nearly two lengths, becoming the sixth Kentucky Derby champion bred at Hamburg Place. After winning the Preakness Stakes two weeks later, he attempted to become the second Triple Crown winner to come from the farm. His bid to become the twelfth Triple Crown winner ended as he finished a listless fourth in the grueling mile-and-a-half Belmont, the third leg of the Triple Crown.

Despite winning over $2 million as a three-year-old, he improved to have an even better four-year-old season. In nine starts, he was a winner seven times, with victories in six Grade 1 Stakes races, including the Breeder's Cup Classic at Churchill Downs. Alysheba retired to Lane's End Farm in Kentucky as the leading money earner of all time, with racing earnings of over $6 million. He held this distinction until his record was broken by Cigar in 1996. Alysheba would be the last thoroughbred champion bred at Hamburg Place.

Thoroughbreds like T.V. Lark and Alysheba brought Hamburg Place back to prominence among horse-racing circles, but the general public knew about Hamburg Place in another capacity beginning in the early 1960s. Preston's wife, Anita, whom he married in 1955, began throwing flamboyant Derby parties at the farm. The parties, always with an audacious theme as a backdrop, became a media event as high-society minglers, actors, celebrities and paparazzi flocked to Hamburg Place every year to participate in the revelry. The party attracted several thousand guests and benefitted several charities, primarily the Bluegrass Boys' Ranch. Never one to worry about what her more conservative Bluegrass neighbors thought, Anita turned Hamburg Place into a raucous and rowdy pre-Derby celebration. In his tell-all book, *Fun While It Lasted*, gambler Bruce McNall remembers an episode at the party:

> *Preston was an extraordinary character whose Derby parties were infamous for drunken debauchery. At one of those parties, Preston led me into his private office where a stunning antique desk dominated the décor. To prove the desk's quality, he poured a couple of shots of bourbon on its top and lit it on fire. When the blaze went out, the desk remained unmarked. With the smell of burnt alcohol hanging in the air, Preston charmed me into buying one of his horses.*[57]

Afterward, McNall remembered, he was taken outside to a swimming pool filled with bubbles and naked women. Whether or not this story is true, the Derby parties hosted by Preston and Anita always pushed the limits acceptable in a conservative region like the Bluegrass.

In the 1980s, Preston and Anita, along with older brother Patrick, began to explore the possibility of selling parcels of Hamburg Place, as Lexington sprawled closer and land values in the region skyrocketed. Several aspects of the property excited developers. First, Hamburg Place is located within the Lexington Urban Services Boundary. First defined in 1957, the Urban Services Boundary, a seventy-three-mile area within Lexington, confines new building activity within its borders. John Madden, when choosing a site for his farm in the late nineteenth century, wanted Hamburg Place to be "only a 15 minute drive in a good roadster"[58] from the Phoenix Hotel, making it all the easier to close business deals. Now the proximity to the city hurdled one potential setback on its path to development. Robert Joice, former long-range planning manager for the Lexington-Fayette Urban County Government, explained, "Once it was decided that the land is within the boundaries, development is considered appropriate."[59]

In 1986, a large shopping center, anchored by a shopping mall, was planned for about one hundred acres of the property. These plans never materialized, but two forces were converging that would forever shape what Hamburg Place was to become. First, Preston and Anita Madden's only son, Patrick, would graduate from Stanford University that same year and come home to attend law school at the University of Kentucky. While at law school, he specialized in real estate development law, becoming an expert in the ins and outs of real estate. It was John Madden's great-grandson Patrick, with energy, drive and business acumen, who would be the driving force in developing the farm. Rather than simply sell the land for development, the Maddens entered into long-term leases with tenants to earn long-term income. The tenant list is formidable: Walmart, Meijer, Lowe's and other who's who of national chain stores. The Hamburg Place that one sees today is largely the vision of Patrick Madden, although the family joke is that "Anita is the idea person, Preston is the detail person, and Patrick gets all the credit."[60] No matter who is in charge, the profits are immense; according to property records, the Maddens have pocketed $65 million in land sales, while also receiving monthly checks from the long-term lease agreements.[61] One member of the Fayette Urban County Planning Commission commented, "Patrick Madden just took it to another level."[62]

The second force in determining Hamburg Place's fate was the building of Interstate 75, and later Man o' War Boulevard, dissecting the farm. Patrick Madden explained that "it didn't make economic sense and it wasn't safe or practical to keep this a horse farm."[63] The interstate, with about seventy-five thousand drivers per day passing by, was the engine behind the development of Hamburg Place. Deals were struck quickly with commercial developers in the late 1990s, with Patrick Madden negotiating the deals himself. He understood the gold mine he was sitting on and that large companies would pay a premium to build there. Quickly, about four hundred acres of the farm were developed. As is true with all suburban sprawl, automobile traffic is key, meaning surface roads were built to accommodate massive amounts of traffic. Sir Barton Way, originally intended as a two-lane road connecting Winchester Road and Man o' War Boulevard, eventually was built with four lanes at Patrick Madden's insistence.

Hamburg Pavilion, about a one-hundred-acre complex, was the first shopping center to be developed at the former horse farm in 1996. Since then, the scope and speed of development shocked, angered or delighted Lexington residents. Several other shopping centers sprouted as well; a thirty-acre complex called Sir Barton Place was built soon after. Then came the largest of all: War Admiral Place, with a Super Walmart and Lowe's, along with many other stores and restaurants, solidifying Hamburg Place as the largest shopping complex in Lexington.

In 2004, Patrick Madden sold 563 acres of the farm to a Tennessee developer, with plans to build three thousand upscale houses. Since then, six residential areas, from upscale housing and single-family houses to town

Old Rosebud Drive at Hamburg Place. *Photo by author.*

homes and apartments have been built. With shopping centers, office parks, residential areas, hotels, restaurants, medical practitioners, parks, schools and even churches, Hamburg Place is literally a city within a city. But there is more to come—much more. Hundreds of acres at Hamburg Place are waiting to be developed with the possibility of a large hospital on the west side of I-75.

Although usually not sentimental about his farm or his horses, one of John Madden's most cherished spots on the property was the equine cemetery. He wanted the public to have access, to "effectually preserve for years to come, as it is my intention to make this spot one of the more interesting areas of Kentucky."[64] The first horse buried was the mare of 1914 Kentucky Derby winner Old Rosebud, Ida Pickwick. Over the years, seventeen more horses, both thoroughbreds and standardbreds, and one polo pony were buried on the plot. Madden's first Derby winner, Plaudit; Sir Martin; Star Shoot; and T.V. Lark are among the horses buried there. In 2005, those eighteen horses lay in the way of space needed for the planned building of the new Super Walmart. Fortunately, the Maddens decided to relocate the cemetery to a spot several hundred yards from the original cemetery. Keeping with the founder of Hamburg Place's intentions, Anita Madden said, "We are trying to reproduce [the cemetery] as close to the original as possible. We want it to be pretty and open all the time."[65]

Wanting to honor the past among the noise and traffic of a shopping center is just one of the ironies of the Madden family, as they have lived, farmed, sold, leased, hosted and profited off the land. Lexington residents are mixed in their reactions to the new version of Hamburg Place. After the War Admiral Shopping Center won an environmental award from the Lexington Environmental Commission, four of the commissioners resigned in protest, one saying, "[Hamburg Place] is one of the worst offenders, the ultimate urban sprawl. Putting flowers on that is like putting make-up on a corpse."[66] Anita Madden herself has played a role in managing growth, serving as a member of the Fayette County Planning and Zoning Commission for seventeen years.

In 2000, the Sierra Club lamented that developing Hamburg Place "had many Lexington residents worried" and "is emblematic of the changes that poorly planned growth is bringing Kentucky."[67] One of those residents was Jack Jones Jr., owner of neighboring Mineola Farm, a thoroughbred operation founded by his grandfather in the 1920s. Residential subdivisions now border one side of the farm, and despite installing thousands of dollars of fencing to protect his horses, Jones struggles with the encroaching development. "It's increasingly difficult to raise expensive horses with dogs and children running onto the property."[68] Jones, while not wanting to sell, eventually wanted his property to be included in the Urban Services Boundary, giving him the option of selling to

John Madden, the "Master of the Turf," in the relocated equine cemetery. *Photo by author.*

Hamburg Place
sprawl. *Photo by
author.*

developers if farming became too difficult. Said neighbor David Demarcus, "With the area around Hamburg Place expanding, it's more logical to put this land up for development than continue farming."[69]

Anita Madden guesses that Hamburg Place will be completely developed to capacity, "depending on the economy, our grandchildren would finish it."[70] That would be six generations of Maddens on the Hamburg Place property. Asked what his great-grandfather would think of what Hamburg Place is today, Patrick Madden was unapologetic: "He was always trading, whether it be land, bloodstock, corporate stocks or whatever."[71] Whether it is breeding sixteen champion racehorses, throwing the most audacious parties in the Bluegrass or developing the farm, the Maddens have always done things in a big way. Today, that is the legacy of the "Master of the Turf" John Madden.

# 7

# BASHFORD MANOR

The Inner Bluegrass Region dominates the thoroughbred breeding industry not only nationally but also within the borders of the commonwealth. The other regions of Kentucky, either not geographically conducive or not established culturally as thoroughbred breeding areas, are not known as thoroughbred hotbeds. But that is not to say that there are no top thoroughbreds from other regions. The 1985 Kentucky Derby winner (and currently holding the distinction of winning in the fifth-fastest time), Spend A Buck, was bred just outside of Owensboro, a city on the Ohio River located in the Pennyroyal Region. On the other side of the state, Charles L. Harrison bred 1911 Kentucky Derby winner Meridian in Bellevue, just across the Ohio River from Cincinnati in northern Kentucky.

The Louisville area claimed several prominent thoroughbred farms in the nineteenth and early part of the twentieth centuries. Brothers John and Hiram Scoggan, although more known for owning horses than breeding them (they owned the talented Proctor Knott), operated a breeding farm outside of Louisville that produced the 1893 Kentucky Derby winner Lookout. A Louisville newspaper article from 1892 observed that "very few Louisville horses have ever started in the Derby. Loftin, Proctor Knott, and Thistle are the only ones I can recall."[72] All three of these horses ran in the 1880s.

The most significant of these Louisville farms was George Long's Bashford Manor, breeder of three Kentucky Derby champions and numerous stakes winners. Although not located in the Inner Bluegrass Region, Bashford

Manor will be included in our narrative for three reasons: 1) the historical significance of the farm, especially in terms of how it related to Kentucky horse racing; 2) the role that suburban sprawl played in its demise as a thoroughbred farm; and 3) the development of the farm, showing that the effects of sprawl are not an isolated problem in the Bluegrass Region but threaten farms all over the commonwealth.

Bashford Manor Farm was founded by James Bennett Wilder in 1874, just outside a small crossroads called Buechel, about six miles from Louisville at the time. Wilder, a director at both the Louisville and Nashville Railroad and the Bank of Louisville, built a three-story French Second Empire–style mansion, a popular architecture style among the wealthy after the Civil War, completing the house in 1871. Wilder named the estate Bashford Manor after an ancestral home in Maryland and the English home of an ancestor.

The story behind the building of the estate is a fascinating one and an important part of Bashford Manor lore. The property already contained a formidable house when Wilder bought the land, but he refused to live in the house because of his hatred toward the former landowner, Paschal D. Craddock. Instead, he dismantled the entire home and used the building materials to build several bridges across Beargrass Creek at various points on the farm. James Bennett Wilder was not the only person in the community who had a problem with the now-deceased Craddock.

Craddock had a sordid reputation, mingling with counterfeiters, horse stealers and thieves. A Louisville newspaper reported that two horses were stolen from the owners of one of the local sawmills and then inexplicably found in hiding at the Craddock home. Later, a herd of six stolen pigs turned up on the Craddock farm. Although Craddock pleaded innocence, his neighbors met at a local schoolhouse and issued a pointed ultimatum:

> *When the conduct of individuals through a series of years is calculated to bring reproach upon neighbors, the right of the citizens to meet together and deliberate as to the mode of acquitting themselves of the reproach and fixing the odium upon the proper objects is unquestionable.*
>
> *Whereas, such is the position of this community with regard to the persons mentioned in the sub-joined resolution, who are associated with and harbor thieves, horse stealers, counterfeiters, and assist them in removing stolen property, especially that stolen from their neighbors; and whereas, legal means have proven ineffective to reach them, Therefore, Resolved, That Paschal D. Craddock…be requested to settle their business and leave the State of Kentucky within six months.*[73]

A subscription was raised as well, offering to buy the property off Craddock at a fair price.

The sixty-five-year-old Craddock ignored the ultimatum and remained on the property. Just two days before the six months' ultimatum expired, a slave named Washington, belonging to prominent citizen and neighbor Andrew Hikes, came to the Craddock property late in the evening, requesting Craddock's presence at his master's residence. His wife begged him not go, but Craddock, being "bold and aggressive by nature," left with the enslaved man. About a quarter mile from his home, on a dark, tree-lined country lane, Craddock was ambushed by three men. The next morning, his body was found in the road, "mutilated by hogs and with three bullet wounds in his thigh."[74] The coroner determined he died from a broken neck after being thrown from his horse.

Washington, Mathew Hike's slave, was brought to trial but was quickly exonerated for lack of evidence. Then, in November, a Mexican War veteran from neighboring Bullitt County named James Miller came forward and confessed that he and two others had killed Craddock at the behest of several prominent men in the community. Among the seven men indicted for murder were Craddock's neighbors, and participants in the above-mentioned ultimatum, Andrew and Frederick Hikes. Most of these neighbors came from prominent families in the community, including the popular Colonel Jack Allen, a local military hero. Still, the public was surprised, although most delighted, when on December 4 all the defendants were acquitted in the murder of Paschal Craddock.

James Bennett Wilder, certainly with social ties and probably business dealings with most of these men, in a show of support for his friends would not live in the same house as Craddock and built a new house—the fifteen-room mansion where he lived until 1888. At that time, he sold the country estate, encompassing 254 acres of rolling farmland, to industrialist George James Long of Louisville, who planned to use it as his summer residence.

George Long was the son of Dennis Long, owner of one of the largest iron pipe foundries in the region, making the elder Long one of the richest men in the city. George followed his father into the lucrative business, eventually serving as vice-president of his father's foundry at the time he bought the Bashford Manor property. Not interested in livestock or farming for commercial reasons, Long began to assemble a thoroughbred racing stable as a hobby—a diversion from his work responsibilities, which must have been considerable. He traveled to Chestnut Hill, Pennsylvania, and purchased bloodstock from the highly regarded Erdenheim stud, after

Bashford Manor, circa 1922. *Courtesy of the Kentucky Derby Museum.*

its owner Norman W. Kittson passed away. The dispersal sale attracted horsemen from all over the country, and Long was not listed as one of the "distinguished breeders" in the November 9, 1888 *New York Times* article describing the dispersal. But Long, with a business partner, Dr. F.E. Corrigan of Louisville, walked away from the sale with the two most expensive stallions on the roster, paying $2,050 and $1,350, respectively.

He brought back to Kentucky no less than a horse whose "speed completely redefined the American Thoroughbred and American racing."[75] This was the nineteen-year-old Alarm. Winning seven times in nine starts, Alarm was "invincible at a mile or less."[76] Although sprinting horses were held in less regard at that time than those that carried their speed over longer distances, Alarm was a much sought-after stallion. He had entered stud in 1874 at James Grinstead's Walnut Hills Farm, south of Lexington, before the much-traveled horse ended up as Bashford Manor's foundation sire. Alarm had already proven himself as a great sire, the best of his get being Himyar, himself an exceptional stallion. Alarm was also a great broodmare sire, being the grandsire of Azra, Manuel and Elwood, all three Kentucky Derby winners. At the Erdenheim dispersal, Long also bought a young stallion named Pardee, a son of Alarm, determined to have the blood of the great stallion at his farm for years to come.

George Long was not one to start small and work his way up. He very quickly began attending horse sales featuring the best-bred thoroughbreds in the country. During the late 1880s and throughout the 1890s, Long's name appears in many New York newspaper listings buying several thoroughbreds at auction. The first listing, from May 1, 1889, shows Long attending a sale held in Lexington for yearlings from three prominent Kentucky thoroughbred farms: Woodburn, Runnymede and Coldstream (formerly McGrathiana) Farms. He walked away with two colts, both sired by the prolific stallion Falsetto.

Falsetto, one of only three horses to sire three Kentucky Derby winners, originally stood at A.J. Alexander's Woodburn Farm. In 1897, the thoroughbred stock at Woodburn was sold, and Falsetto was purchased by George Long and brought to Bashford Manor. Falsetto was already advanced in years and only lived at Bashford Manor for seven years. In July 1904, the *New York Times* reported that Falsetto, "one of the Kings of the Turf, is dying of pneumonia at George Long's farm."[77] The twenty-eight-year-old stallion died just a few weeks later and was buried on the farm.

While Long assembled his breeding bloodstock, he also put together an impressive racing stable, mainly racing at the "western tracks" (west at this time meaning Kentucky, Ohio, Illinois and Louisiana). Periodically, he sent horses east to challenge the more powerful eastern stables in the prestigious stakes offerings in New York, New Jersey and Maryland. The gamble to begin his breeding operation with the blood of Alarm paid off very quickly in 1892, when a daughter of Alarm named Albia produced a Kentucky Derby winner named Azra. Albia was one of the two broodmares Long had acquired at the Erdenheim dispersal in 1888. Although Azra only beat two other horses in the race, it was a thrilling finish, with Azra coming from six lengths back to beat Ed Corrigan's Huron by a nose. Many in the crowd thought the victory was due to the superior ride by African American jockey Alonzo Clayton, who, it was said, "worked like a demon"[78] and "practically carried Azra the last few jumps" to win the race by scant inches.

The victory in the Kentucky Derby must have been a source of pride for George Long, as the year before he had entered his first Derby horse, Hart Wallace, only to see him finish last in the slowest Kentucky Derby ever run. Azra had the distinction of being the first Louisville-bred horse to win the Derby.

Azra would prove his mettle later in the year against better competition by winning the more prestigious Travers Stakes at Saratoga, as well as in front of the home folks in the Clark Stakes at Churchill Downs. He was retired at the end of his three-year-old season, with earnings of $20,710. Unfortunately, he never had a chance to prove himself as a stallion. While preparing the horse for his stud career at Bashford Manor, he was stabled at Latonia Racetrack in Northern Kentucky. Trainer John Morris gave a supper for several sportsmen at the stable and afterward instructed a groom to bring out of the stall what he called "the finest young stallion in America." Soon after Azra was put back into his stall, a stable hand "rushed up to Mr. Morris with the bad news that Azra was down in his stall and couldn't get up." A veterinarian was called immediately, but the news was devastating—Azra had "ruptured himself" and would be dead by morning.[79]

Azra was not just a racehorse to the Long family but also an endeared member of the family. After his Kentucky Derby victory, George Long's young son Irving was spotted at his grandfather's house, "gotten up in a blue suit and jockey cap on his fair hair; he rode about his grandfather's lot on his bicycle, stopping every now and then, to regale the neighbors with a thrilling description of the great race." Dennis Long, George's father, never took the slightest interest in horses or racing but was "beside himself with excitement when the Bashford colors were raised."[80] Upon receiving the telephone call that Azra only had a few hours to live, Mrs. Long called the news "a grievous shock" and recalled "having her arms around his neck many a time."[81]

After Azra's 1892 Derby victory, Long ran horses in three successive Kentucky Derby contests, finishing second with Plutus, third with Sigurd and fourth with Curator. In 1896, another grandson of Alarm was born, named Manuel. Long campaigned Manuel for much of his two-year-old season, but although the colt showed some promise, he only won a disappointing three of seventeen starts. Because of his potential and good bloodline, Long was still able to sell Manuel for $15,000. Manuel only raced four times as a three-year-old, winning once. That win put him in the history books, however; it was the twenty-fifth running of the Kentucky Derby. Earlier in the year, he had fallen in a race in Memphis, injuring his leg. In his victory in the Derby, it was reported that he exacerbated the injury even more and was forced to take time off to heal. The injury must have been more severe than first thought, as he was sold again, this time for only $500 at a horse sale at Morris Park in New Jersey. He died in obscurity soon after.

In 1900, Long had another good one in a horse named Hindus. Although Hindus ran last every step of the way in the Kentucky Derby, Long took his three-year-old colt to Gravesend in New York to run in the Preakness Stakes. Long's faith in his horse proved well founded, as Hindus came from far back to win. It should be noted that none of the competition he faced in Kentucky Derby shipped east to run in the Preakness that year. It should also be noted that the New York media wasn't ready to credit the talent of the western invader Hindus but rather the "bungling ride"[82] of the jockey on the favored Samaritan.

George Long's best racehorse bred at Bashford Manor was foaled in 1903 and was named after a knight in Charlemagne's court. His name was Sir Huon. Sir Huon was the culmination of Long's breeding plan at his farm, many years in the making. Sir Huon's sire was the prolific Falsetto, known for producing runners with a plethora of stamina, while his dam was Ignite, grand dam of Alarm, which would instill speed. (Ignite was also the dam of Long's Preakness winner Hindus.) What resulted was, by many accounts, an especially beautiful and perfectly conformed bay horse. George Long's son, Irving, called Sir Huon the most beautiful horse he ever saw, while the *Courier Journal* called him "the grandest looking three year old thoroughbred that has been seen in this, the home of the horse, in twenty years."[83]

Not only was Sir Huon beautiful, but he also lived up to his impeccable breeding. He raced nine times as a two-year-old, including a sprint win at Saratoga against some of the top eastern two-year-olds. A big colt, Sir Huon was still developing into his powerful body, signaling that his best days were to come. As a juvenile, Long was offered $17,000 for the colt, but he insisted on $20,000, which was refused. Sir Huon was held out of the races until May 2, to give him more time to both physically and mentally develop, when he made his three-year-old debut in the Kentucky Derby. Despite the lack of experience, the bettors were swayed by the hometown horse's regal looks and fast workout times. Sir Huon was made a slight favorite over Charles Ellison's entry of the talented filly Lady Navarre and James Reddick. The largest Derby crowd up to that time saw a game Sir Huon fight off a late challenge by the filly to win by two lengths. The newspaper headline the next day, clearly ecstatic at the victory by the hometown horse, pronounced, "The King is even Greater than the Queen! Long Live the King!"[84]

George Long watched the race unfold from the Churchill Downs infield with his family, including daughter Anna, who and had been released from Norton Infirmary specifically to see their magnificent horse run. While the crowd, the press and the rest of the family celebrated the great victory, George Long "maintained his dignity throughout. He may have wanted to throw his hands up in the air but he did not. Mr. Long has been there before which may account for his restraint." Another newspaper description described Long as *a rather heavy set, pleasant faced man, whose hair is tinged with gray, saw the race from the center of the infield. He stood at the highest point of the emerald lawn and watched with a critical eye every foot of the journey. When it was ended his only remark was "I thought he would do it."* [85]

Irving Long, by now attending Purdue University and a member of the football team, was not as composed. An undated and untitled article found in a scrapbook belonging to George Long relates:

*While standing in the paddock, he [Irving] was asked what he thought of his horse's chances. Nervously, but fondly patting the horse...he said "I don't think we can lose. He is the greatest horse I ever saw and we expect great things from him today and hereafter." As time passed, Irving began to display considerable nervousness...the boy who had faced without a flinch some of the most stalwart gridiron warriors of the west, was visibly affected, pale and trembling. When the race was run and his horse was returned the winner, he could scarcely speak, but the tears in his eyes...betrayed his emotion and happiness.*

Sir Huon continued his winning ways, beating Lady Navarre again in a match race, as they were the only two to show up for the Latonia Derby. After a victory in the Queen City Stakes, again at Latonia, Sir Huon was shipped to Sheepshead Bay to compete against the eastern horses in the Commonwealth Stakes. Unimpressed with Sir Huon's credentials, gamblers sent him off as a fifteen-to-one long shot. The large bay shocked the crowd by rallying from far back to snatch victory at the wire.

New Yorkers would not make the same mistake twice. Two weeks later, in the Sea Gate Stakes at Brighton Beach Racetrack, he was made three-to-one favorite and easily won the race in the mud. This victory stamped Sir Huon as possibly the best racehorse in America. Unfortunately, Sir Huon sustained an injury at Saratoga in the Saratoga Cup (still finishing second) and was never the same. He ran once as a four-year-old and once at age five but was unable to regain his previous superior form. He was retired in 1908 and sent to stud at Bashford Manor, with earnings of almost $40,000. It was a disappointing ending for a solid racing career cut short by injury.

With Sir Huon's incredible Falsetto-Ignite pedigree, there were high hopes for him as a sire. Unfortunately, this son of Falsetto was not an outstanding stallion of racehorses himself. He lived at Bashford Manor until 1918, when he embarked on another aspect of his breeding career.

In October of that year, while World War I raged in Europe, the Maryland Jockey Club contacted George Long regarding the possibility of running a horse in the Remount Purse, a novel contest in which the contestants were thoroughbreds owned by the government and ridden by army officers in full uniform.

George Long's farm manger, W.S. Hopkins, wrote to the club that "they regretted that they had no stallion of proper age to run for the Purse…but they had at Bashford Manor a stallion of high quality, a Kentucky Derby winner, which they were ready to turn over to the government on the occasion of the first Breeders' Remount Purse."[86] Sir Huon, with his near-perfect confirmation and easygoing temperament, proved to be an excellent stallion for the army, siring horses suited to cavalry purposes.

Long had many other talented thoroughbreds over the thirty-four years he was involved in the sport. These included 1916 Kentucky Oaks winner Kathleen, his best filly. He also campaigned Sir Cleges, which probably would have won the 1908 Kentucky Derby if the weather had cooperated. Disliking mud, the favored horse ran second to Stone Street on a deep, muddy Churchill Downs racetrack.

The last Bashford Manor horse to compete in the hometown Kentucky Derby was Free Lance, which ran well for a mile but tired the last quarter mile to finish fourth to Worth in 1912. Free Lance met an untimely death as a stallion at Bashford Manor. A farmworker forgot to latch a gate, allowing Ralph, another stallion, access to the younger and smaller stallion's paddock. The two stallions fought to the death. Ralph came away with many lacerations, and Free Lance was dead.

Long's health began to decline in the early 1920s, and it was decided to sell all of his bloodstock at a dispersal sale at the farm in August 1922. A total of seventy-six head of horse were sold, marking the end of Bashford Manor Farm as a major breeding operation in American racing. George Long died in his Louisville business office on January 15, 1930, of heart disease at the age of seventy-seven.

Unlike the other subjects of this narrative, George Long did not look at thoroughbred racing as a business. His business was iron making and, later, serving as president of the Interstate Water Company, as well as serving on boards for various organizations. Thoroughbred racing, to him, was a diversion from the pressures of the boardroom and the role he played in the industrialization of the region. He owned no other livestock on his farm; his only interest was as a sportsman. Long served on the Kentucky State Racing Commission for a number of years, as well as on the board of directors at

Churchill Downs. In 1902, a stakes race for two-year-old colts was named the Bashford Manor Stakes, a race still run at the present time.

Unlike other racing owners and breeders of the time, Long was not a gambler. According to one newspaper account, "It is reliably reported that the maximum limit of a single bet is $10."[87] While this may or may not be true, Long certainly enjoyed playing poker. One tradition was to play on a small island in the middle of a rock-lined lake on the Bashford Manor property. Long hosted all-day poker parties every Fourth of July.

The small island anecdote gives a glimpse of what the property must have looked like a century ago. Beside the pastoral, rock-lined pool, with access provided by a wooden bridge, stood one of the largest barns in the state. Two huge, oval-shaped windows stood at one end, letting in natural light. The barn even had a full basement underneath and, according to a Louisville newspaper, "about two acres of roof on the place."[88] An ivy-covered icehouse and smokehouse, as well as several other smaller barns, graced the property. A two-story carriage house stood to the right and just behind the mansion. The grounds also contained a waterworks, a gas plant and "every convenience of modern equipment."

An interesting note in the farm dispersal advertisement in 1922 was the innocuous detail that Bashford Manor was located only two miles from the city of Louisville. An aerial photo of the estate, taken that same year, shows the property still very rural in character. However, during the thirty-four years that George Long lived at the country estate, the city kept inching ever closer along the Bardstown Pike (later Bardstown Road) corridor. Louisville was on its way.

After Long's death, the estate stayed in the family until 1951, when it began to be subdivided. The mansion and a small portion of the land were bought by the Buechel Women's Club, which hoped to restore the home. The club used the house for its meetings, as well as renting the opulent mansion for weddings and receptions. In 1956, the movie *Raintree County*, starring Elizabeth Taylor and Montgomery Clift in a Civil War–era film, was partially filmed on the property.

Soon after the women's club purchased the mansion, most of the farmland went under the shovel, as the 1950s' urban sprawl phenomenon brought the city to Bashford Manor. Residential subdivisions called Bashford Manor Gardens and Manorview replaced rolling farmland in 1952. In 1954, the largest subdivision, Village Green, was built. Also at this time, the City of Louisville proposed to annex the area, eying the substantial property tax contributions of the young families in the new subdivisions. It was incorporated into the city of Louisville in 1953.

# Bashford Manor

Bashford Manor development. *Photo by author.*

With hundreds of young families moving into the area, the area began to change drastically. The Watterson Expressway, a twenty-two-mile loop around the city, was built in the late 1950s, just north of Bashford Manor's property line. This gave the Bashford Manor area easier access to the city—and gave the city easier access to the countryside. Bardstown Road was widened to meet the demands of congestion, stoplights were installed and traffic filled the roads as the Bashford Manor area became one of the most popular places to settle for young couples.

Commercial developments sprang up to meet the needs of the growing population of the subdivisions. A movie theater, originally a twin cinema, was built and would expand until, in the 1970s, it was the largest movie theater in the state, boasting sixteen screens and seating six thousand people. In 1970, a large shopping center was announced, and the destruction of Bashford Manor Farm began. Headlines announced that "Horse Barns Have to Go," and in a matter of weeks, the demolition was complete, leaving only the aging mansion and carriage house, looking out of place and vulnerable surrounded by construction. Citing the expense of the upkeep on the rock-lined swimming pool, it was plowed under. Parts of the largest barn were saved; horse stalls were donated to a local riding club, and the two huge oval windows were salvaged. By 1973, the fifty-six-thousand-square-foot, horse-themed Bashford Manor Shopping Mall stood in its place, welcoming shoppers from around the region.

The new mall anchored a thriving suburban business district, and the land the mansion sat on was looked at as prime real estate. The Buechel Women's Club had bought the estate for $25,000 in 1951; in 1972, it sold the mansion and one acre of surrounding land for $142,500. Of course, the mansion was more of a hindrance; the value was in the land. The buyer was the Louisville Trust Bank, which built a branch on a corner of the property. The next year, the house came back into the Long family's possession, as two of George Long's grandson's, J. Royden Peabody Jr. and D. Irving Long, purchased the home with the intention of reselling it to restaurant chains. These plans did not materialize, and the grand mansion was demolished in 1973.

The French Second Empire mansion stood on the property at Bashford Manor for just over a century. The Bashford Manor Mall, with its eighty-five stores, only lasted thirty-one years. As the 1950s subdivisions aged and the suburban sprawl spread farther into the county, the demographics of the area began to depress economically. Large tenants of the mall abandoned the area for greener pastures—newer sprawl located farther from the city's core—until 2003, when one lone store remained. Later that year, a large section of the mall was demolished to make way for new development. Two years later, the rest of the once-thriving mall fell to the wrecking ball. The Bashford Manor Mall had become a victim of what had given it life: suburban sprawl.

In its place came the ultimate symbol of unchecked suburban sprawl: Walmart. The national retailer believed that the location was still desirable for retail but needed a new concept. "The direction of the property has changed from an enclosed mall revival to a 'Power Center' concept."[89] The store was completed and opened in 2004, adding another chapter in the land of Bashford Manor. Quickly, more stores, banks and restaurants followed Walmart's lead, hastening a road expansion that had been planned years earlier.

The results of sprawl are easy to see when one visits today's Bashford Manor. Chain stores, traffic congestion, pollution, noise, water drainage problems and everything else that sprawl entails are a part of today's Bashford Manor. Beargrass Creek, once a picturesque stream running through the farm property, is now a mere dumping ground for trash. In 2009, volunteers

Bashford Manor's memorial to its three Kentucky Derby winners. *Photo by author.*

pulled out mattresses, box springs, hubcaps, bedposts, many pounds of trash and about forty shopping carts. These are the pollutants that one can see, but just as devastating are the invisible pollutants draining into the creek from the blacktop runoff.

Today, the city of Louisville stretches miles past Bashford Manor. Much of the sprawl that destroyed Bashford Manor Farm has itself been demolished and replaced by fancier, newer sprawl—sprawl with catchy names, like large box stores as "Super Centers" and subdivisions as "Lifestyle Centers." And it continues, relatively unchecked, farther and farther down the Bardstown Road corridor, eating up valuable and sometimes historic farmland along the way. Bashford Manor was the greatest, and the last, of the major thoroughbred breeding farms in Louisville.

# 8

# THE FIGHT TO SAVE
# THE BLUEGRASS

The first effort to save the Bluegrass Region happened by accident. During the 1950s, as Lexington suburbs grew, there were a few people in the community who understood the ramifications of unchecked growth. But the thinking in Lexington was like in most places: growth symbolized progress, and vitality and rural lands would have to be sacrificed for the good of the community. In 1958, Lexington became the first city in the nation to create and install an Urban Services Boundary (also called an Urban Growth Boundary), effectively limiting growth outside city limits. The boundary was not created to save the surrounding farms but as a health concern due to an overhaul of the city's sewer system. With high hepatitis rates and raw sewage in the streets due to an overtaxed sewer system, the Urban Services Boundary was created to alleviate that problem. Out of Fayette County's total 285 square miles, the boundary encircled 69 square miles of the city's core. Without intending to, the government saved hundreds of acres of land from development, including many prominent thoroughbred farms.

In an article for the Lincoln Institute of Land Policy, Arthur C. Nelson writes that at its core, an Urban Services Boundary serves two basic purposes. First (and the reason Lexington's was originally implemented), "to promote compact, contiguous and accessible development provided with efficient public services."[90] Second, "to preserve open space, agricultural land, and environmentally sensitive areas that are not currently suitable for development."[91] For whichever reason, and usually for both, other cities soon followed Lexington's lead, as virtually every city in America had to come to terms with suburban sprawl. In 1973, the State of Oregon made urban growth boundaries mandatory in each city's comprehensive land-use plans. Other states have since followed.

Despite the installation of Lexington's boundary in 1958, several historic and culturally significant horse farms were lost, including the already mentioned McGrathiana and Hamburg Place, both located inside the boundary line and both developed in various forms within the confines of existing laws. Other farms were developed as well, one of the most prominent being Hal Price Headley's four-thousand-acre showpiece, Beaumont Farm, which became office, business and residential space in the 1990s. These farms were seen by many as simply sitting too close to the city's core and worth the sacrifice for a growing Lexington to prosper.

Developer Patrick Madden, great-grandson of Hamburg Place founder John Madden and the man responsible for much of the development of that property, shrugs off criticism within the community for the development of Hamburg Place. Yet Madden himself supports the concept of an Urban

Residential area, formerly Beaumont Farm. *Photo by author.*

Services Boundary as a means to limit growth in rural areas. "I think Lexington has the best mechanism in place to prevent urban sprawl."[92]

Since it was put in place, the boundary lines of the area have been controversial. Developers claim that limiting where growth can occur drives up land prices, limiting those who can afford to purchase a house and live the American dream. They claim that it is simply supply-and-demand economics and should not be regulated by the government. Attorney Bruce Simpson, arguing for Lexington developers, claimed that "lack of acreage to develop makes land expensive…It makes the cost of living more expensive because you're paying more for land than you can pay elsewhere in other counties."[93]

Opponents of expanding the boundary point out that there is always plenty of land within the boundary that is undeveloped. Rather than building outward, infill and redevelopment of the urban areas inside the boundary should be emphasized.

In 1996, an expansion was made to the boundary line, with about fifty-three hundred acres (about 8.5 square miles), mainly in the east and southeast, added to Urban Services Boundary. The area was quickly developed, and the demand for more land to become available for development made newspaper headlines. Citizens differed in opinion over how far the boundary line should be expanded and into what areas it should expand.

Also in the late 1990s, the debate about minimum lot sizes in rural Fayette County caused an outbreak of concern. A proposal to the planning commission, creating fifty-acre-minimum lot sizes, sparked a deluge in ten-acre tract surrounding the Urban Services Boundary, the minimum lot size at the time. In response, the minimum lot size was changed in 1999 to forty acres from the previous minimum of ten acres. With the passing of the change in zoning, this drastically constrained who could build and what could be built on undeveloped land in rural Fayette County. Critics countered that building on forty acres of pristine, Kentucky bluegrass was out of the reach financially for most people—which was the point, to a certain degree. Ten-acre tracts of land were rural estates; large forty-acre tracts were not desirable to most people, unless they were interested in putting the land toward agricultural use.

The year 2006 proved to be a controversial one for the boundary, as five property owners, owning eighteen hundred contiguous acres of farmland east and southeast of the city, banded together to ask the city for inclusion inside the boundary. Their farms sat very close to development, and were "in the path of growth already coming out of Hamburg Place."[94] The attorneys for the landowners tried to make inclusion more palatable to the public by stressing that, by being included all at one time, development "would allow for more careful planning and thoughtful development."[95] Another reason they thought inclusion should be allowed was that the farms were home to cattle and hayfields but not thoroughbreds.

Other farms became involved in the argument, most being farms located on the boundary line separating rural from urban. Jack Jones Jr., owner of Mineola Farm, who was tired of the encroachment of a neighboring subdivision, applied to the planning commission to be included within the boundary. Although the farm had been in his family since the 1920s, Jones wanted inclusion "to give him options."[96] Another farm that wanted inclusion was Eaton Farm, also bordering the boundary. The threat of light industry being developed on an adjacent farm, and within the boundary, prompted the request. The Eaton Farm manager said, "If that farm is ever developed as light industry, we would like the option, far down the road, to do the same."[97]

A stormy debate ensued. Neighbors came out in force opposing the expansion of the boundary, and the plans to expand were scrapped. But the controversy did not end with this decision. Later that year, in a comprehensive land-use plan, about seventy-seven hundred acres of farmland, once again mainly to the east and southeast of the city, were designated as "reserve land." This reserve land was not open for immediate development but would be the first to go once the boundary was expanded at a later date. In January 2007, this "urban reserve" concept was defeated in a vote by commission members. *Bloodhorse* magazine reported that "most attendees burst into applause"[98] when the decision was announced. It was cited as a victory for those wanting to focus growth within the confines of the boundary, with the urban reserve concept possibly accelerating the process of allowing growth outside of it.

Expanding the urban service area—when to expand, where to expand and how far to expand—brings up questions that will continually be a source of controversy among Fayette County residents. One advantage that Lexington enjoyed when dealing with these questions was its merging of city and county governments, which took place in 1974, becoming the first city in Kentucky, and one of the first nationally, to do so. Lexington writer Tom Eblen notes in his June 20, 2008 "Bluegrass and Beyond" blog that this "made services more efficient, and sidestepped annexation fights and turf battles that plague other cities and counties." But while this process is more streamlined, the fact remains that property owners with land bordering the

Urban Services Boundary line are under constant pressure to be included in the boundary as well, whether or not it is designated reserved land.

While the debate was raging over the Urban Services Boundary line, a land survey conducted by the city noted that there were fifty-six hundred acres available for residential development *within* the Urban Services Boundary. Nevertheless, home builders, still building to the suburban style of decades past, threatened that if the boundary line was not expanded, they would build in neighboring counties that did not have constraints like those in Fayette County. Tom Kelley, president of the Homebuilders Association of Lexington, claimed, "Builders in Fayette County tell me they are going to have to go to adjoining counties…if it isn't expanded."[99] And other neighboring counties, none with large cities, none with Urban Service Boundaries but all with growing populations, responded largely with open arms to the developers.

In 2000, at the same time it implemented its minimum lot size from ten to forty acres, Fayette County government launched a bold program to protect the outlying farmland. The Purchase of Developmental Rights (PDR) program provided government-funded conservation easements to agricultural properties, protecting them in perpetuity from development. While they were a novel idea in Kentucky at the time, PDR programs have been used in environmentally sensitive areas in the United States since the early 1970s.

Four goals were listed for the program when it was launched in 2000: 1) purchase conservation easements to protect 50,000 acres (out of 128,267 acres in the rural service area) over the next twenty years; 2) protect the agricultural and horse economies of Fayette County by conserving large areas of farmland; 3) conserve and protect the natural, scenic open space and historic and agricultural resources of rural Fayette County; and 4) protect the tourism economy of Fayette County by preserving the unique character and "sense of place" that attracts visitors from all over the world. It was also noted that 50,000 acres only represented 27 percent of all land in Fayette County.[100]

All farms have three types of monetary values: the intrinsic value, referring to the sum of all of the parts (the residence, the outbuildings, the timber, the land, etc); the agricultural use value, referring to, basically, what the farmer makes on profit from selling his product; and the future development value, referring to what the property's value would be in the future. In the PDR process, once an independent agent conducts an appraisal, the landowner is made an offer, and if accepted, the property may not be developed—the landowner has sold that aspect of the property. The landowner, however, continues to farm the property and retain the economic profits of the land. The easement is binding on the property after the owner relinquishes ownership.

Conservation easements—a voluntary, legally binding agreement made between the landowner and, in this case, the government—have been instrumental in curbing development and preserving coveted land and its resources. The government, through a variety of funding sources, including general appropriations, bonds and state and federal monies, pays the difference between the current unrestricted value of the land and the value as restricted by a conservation easement at the time of appraisal.

Of course, funding is key for the program to work, but one reason funding has remained strong from different levels of government is because farmland preservation and conservation are seen as matters of national security. Conserved farmland is a base for our nation's food supply, and that supply is and will continue to be stressed as other developing nations need additional farmland to feed their populations. While no one would argue that conserving farmland that is home to thoroughbreds is a question of national security, the economic benefits of the thoroughbred industry to Kentucky greatly outweigh the investment of government money into the PDR program.

To qualify for the PDR program in Fayette County, a point system called the Land Evaluation and Site Assessment (LESA) is used to prioritize which farms are to be conserved. Points are awarded for such environmental factors as  parcel size, length of public road frontage, proximity of land already under easement protection, soil quality, farm activity, agricultural improvements, environmentally sensitive areas and historic or cultural resources. Points are subtracted if the land is near or bordering the Urban Services Boundary.

The benefits of the programs are many. For one, farmers are made a cash payment for the developmental rights, in many cases helping to fund retirement (if not paying debts) or to expand or buy additional land or new equipment. Many farmers are "land rich" but "cash poor," so the cash payment for the development rights can be a godsend.

Although critics claim that the program favors large thoroughbred farms, as of 2010, the breakdown of the 141 farms under PDR protection did not support this claim. Seventy-nine of the farms were equine (not all thoroughbred), 51 general agriculture and 11 classified as "other" (sod, trees, historic). Certainly, large thoroughbred operations benefit from the program, and many of them are prioritized due to their ranking on the LESA point system, but the other types of farms have, as evidenced by the numbers above, refuted that criticism. Despite criticism and a struggling economy at the beginning of the twenty-first century, the program continues to be a success by most standards. Other counties, also facing similar sprawl problems, have emulated Fayette County's program. Bluegrass Region neighbor to the north, Scott County, implemented a similar program in 2008.

Fayette County's Purchase of Development Rights protects several well-known historic horse farms. Bluegrass Heights Farm, located just outside of Lexington, was one of the first farms under development protection from the PDR program. H.N. Davis founded the farm in 1911 and raised saddle horses, hemp and mules. The second generation of the family began breeding thoroughbreds. It was a good choice, as two Kentucky Derby winners, Black Gold (1924) and Burgoo King (1932), were bred on the farm. "We're trying to draw the line so [development] doesn't jump over our heads and go on," said farm owner Colonel Horace N. Davis.[101] Although Bluegrass Heights sits right on the Urban Services Boundary border, and that would be a negative in the LESA priority system, the fact that two Derby winners were bred there made it an important farm to save.

In 2008, Bluegrass Heights was sold to Padua Stables, owned by Satish Sanan, who outsourced its management to Three Chimneys Farm. After purchasing the 275-acre property, whose developmental rights are firmly guaranteed by the PDR program, Sanan said, "We will be undertaking a major construction project to bring the property up to world-class standards while respecting the historical significance of the wonderful old structures that are within the property."[102]

Unfortunately, across the street from Bluegrass Heights, and located just within the Urban Services Boundary, there is development where there once stood another historic farm. Glenridge Farm, originally the home of 1998 Kentucky Derby winner Real Quiet, is gone.

The PDR program received an important historic property in 2005, enlisting the former Indian Hill Farm into the easement program. Named after an Adena Indian mound, the 270-acre farm, under the guidance of Lee Eaton, bred many prominent thoroughbreds. The 1976 Kentucky Derby and Belmont Stakes winner Bold Forbes was bred on the farm in 1973.

The farm also contains a cemetery of the graves of the original owners of the property. Founded by Charles C. Moore and his wife, Maryanne, the couple had three daughters. One of the daughters was married to Major

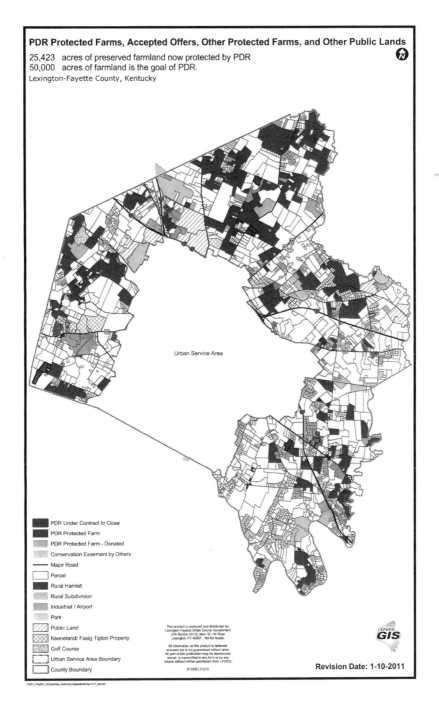

Purchase of Development Rights map. *Courtesy of the Lexington-Fayette Urban County Government.*

Thomas Y. Brent, a cavalry officer with the Fifth Kentucky Cavalry, CSA. He was killed at the Battle of Green River Bridge in Kentucky on July 4, 1863. All are buried in a small family plot on the farm. The PDR program focuses on land preservation, but many times so much more is preserved.

Certainly, without the Urban Services Boundary and the conservative handling of its expansion since its inception, Lexington and Fayette County would look much different than they do today. Residential neighborhoods would no doubt fill acre after acre of much of rural Fayette County. But Lexington's forward thinking on land use, establishing an Urban Services Boundary in 1958 and raising the minimum lot size to forty acres in 1999 had consequences—or advantages, depending on your perspective—for neighboring counties with less stringent development demands. The sprawl that would have spilled out into rural Fayette County instead congested northern Jessamine, western Clark and northern Madison Counties. Since there is no uniform land-use management program for the entire eight counties that compose the Inner Bluegrass Region, each county decides its own policies. After years of watching their own rural counties turn into extensions of Lexington sprawl, some of the neighboring counties began to enact stricter land-use policies with mixed success.

The counties surrounding Fayette County exploded with population growth, as these counties were seen as more hospitable to development and more willing to sell off farmland to build residential and commercial properties without the constraints found in Fayette County. Jessamine County, with the county seat of Nicholasville only nine miles southwest of Lexington, quickly felt the onslaught of a growing population, exploding from 39,041 in 2000, to almost 47,000 in 2010. The mainly rural county has a history of top thoroughbred farms, including Almahurst (today called the Ramsey Farm), which is where legendary thoroughbred racehorse Exterminator was born in 1915.

Although there are no interstates in Jessamine County, its border with Fayette County has built up rapidly with residential subdivisions to meet the demands of the growing population. While sustaining high population growth, Jessamine County added few jobs within the county, creating a shortfall. Over half of Jessamine County's workers clog the mostly two-lane arteries heading toward Lexington five days a week, leaving Jessamine County—and leaving their payroll taxes in Fayette County. "They leave their payroll taxes in other counties, but return home each evening with expectations of a high level of community benefits."[103] One other advantage for developers in Jessamine County, but adding fuel to the fire, it boasts a small minimum lot size for rural development, only five acres, making development much more attainable.

One county to the north of Fayette County lies Scott County, which saw massive residential population growth with the building of a Toyota manufacturing plant in the late 1980s. In April 2007, just after Fayette County voted not to extend its Urban Services Boundary, a proposal to build thirty-one houses on fifty-nine acres on a portion of Crestwood Farm in Scott County raised eyebrows and sparked angry comments from neighbors. Sitting on the Scott-Fayette County border, Crestwood Farm, owned by the Pope McLean family, spreads over five hundred acres along the county's border. The McLean family has been a respected part of the thoroughbred community for several generations, with Pope McLean Jr. an appointee for the Thoroughbred Charities of America Board. The McLeans are not first-generation Bluegrass farmers, nor are they absentee landowners. The farm was home to several outstanding runners, including champion Serena's Song and 1994 Kentucky Oaks winner Sardula.

But the announcement caused a wave of reaction by outspoken neighbors concerned with the possible development of the farm. "It's everybody's right to do what they want to do, but why are you in the horse business if you're going to develop horse farm land that will potentially cause a domino effect?" asked neighbor Joe Clay of Runnymede Farm, the oldest family horse farm in Kentucky. Clay expressed what so many were thinking as they saw so much prime farmland being developed throughout the region: "Everybody has to be committed to trying to preserve this land."[104]

The ensuing arguments before the Scott County Planning Commission highlighted several environmental problems. "The farm is smack in the middle of the horse farm belt,"[105] said neighbor and Antebellum Farm owner Chris Newton. Lack of storm sewers was cited, as was the property's inclusion of environmentally sensitive areas. Furthermore, the development would cause neighboring properties to diminish in value and add congestion to the narrow roads in the area.

The Georgetown-Scott County Planning Commission met the next month to decide on the proposal. After a heated three-hour debate, the proposal was accepted on four-to-three vote. Pope Mclean was not surprised at the approval, noting that "it was approved because it was totally compliant."[106] McLean also asserted that there were no immediate plans to develop the property but that the family was simply securing their property rights, which they did within the confines of the Scott County zoning laws. "I love this industry," contends Pope McLean Jr. "This is what we make our living on, and we're in it for the long haul. But we also have to protect our interests. No one knows what the future holds for this industry…For a farmer, the land is a major asset, and in some regards is like a retirement plan."[107]

In 2009, Scott County became the second Kentucky county to adopt a Purchase of Development Rights program as sprawl gobbled up farmland at a rapid rate. The successful Fayette County PDR program was largely adapted by Scott County to expedite implementation. The program's original goal was to preserve 20 percent of the agricultural zoned land, with an annual goal of two thousand acres. As of this writing, the program is still in its developmental stage.

Woodford County, bordering Fayette to the west, features many historic and well-known thoroughbred farms, ranking second only to Fayette County in number of farms. Not only is there a large quantity of farms, but also the quality is impressive. Driving east toward Lexington on Highway 60, one sees some of the most majestic, well-known and successful farms in racing history. Lane's End, Adena Springs, Three Chimneys and Ashford are all located along this corridor within Woodford County.

Woodford County is also between the state capital of Frankfort and Lexington, making it an appealing community for workers in both cities. Like other counties, Woodford, with its county seat of Versailles, responded by first creating a minimum rural lot size for most of the county at forty acres. Urban service boundaries were implemented for the towns of Versailles and Midway. Woodford County has also been outspoken for the need for all of the Inner Bluegrass Region counties to work together, in uniform, to create policies that do not create winners and losers in the fight against sprawl.

This has been proven difficult to accomplish. Although it is easy to combine all the Inner Bluegrass Region counties together for the sake of marketing or tourism, each county within the region has its own economic goals and agendas. Differences in culture, transportation, geography, soil, economic history and urbanization all contribute to how each county decides the best uses for its land. The far eastern county within the region, Madison, has six interstate exchanges along Interstate 75. Jessamine County has none. This alone greatly affects how each county will use large parcels of its land and what kind of zoning regulations will be put into place.

Despite efforts to control sprawl within the region—some counties are very aggressive and some are not—land development tore through the region at a very rapid pace. In Fayette County alone, despite the constraints put into place, from 1997 to 2002, it lost 19,508 agricultural acres to development. Other surrounding Bluegrass counties showed similar, if not more, alarming statistics. Finally, in 2006, the world was alerted to what many concerned Bluegrass Region citizens already knew: Kentucky's famed thoroughbred industry was seriously threatened by suburban sprawl. Four groups within the region—the Kentucky Heritage Council, the University of Kentucky's College of Design, the Bluegrass Conservancy and the Bluegrass Trust for Historic Preservation—banded together and nominated the region for inclusion in the World Monuments Fund "watch list" of endangered landscapes. Marty Hylton, of the World Monument Fund said, "Of all the sites on the 2006 watch list, the Inner Bluegrass has received the most press next to Iraq and New Orleans/Gulf Coast."[108] Public outcry across the nation was loud and clear.

Upon learning that their nomination to the World Monuments Fund watch list was accepted, the four collaborating organizations issued statements expressing their bittersweet satisfaction of inclusion. David Mohny, dean of the College of Agriculture at the University of Kentucky said, "Being named to this list recognizes what those of us who live here already understand—that the central Kentucky Bluegrass is a world-class, world-renowned landscape worthy of preservation."[109]

David L. Morgan, executive director of the Kentucky Heritage Council and State Historic Preservation Officer, noted:

> Addressing the urgent and long-term challenges that impact this region begins with increased awareness and a clear understanding of the value that these cultural and historic resources bring to the economy and heritage of Kentucky...Unfortunately, people often view preservation as being anti-growth and anti-development but that is a common and troubling misperception. Preservation is about identifying landscapes or buildings that are a part of our history and working together to find ways to keep them sustainable.[110]

Tracee de Han, executive director for the Bluegrass Trust for Preservation, said:

> As part of our goal of nominating the Bluegrass Cultural landscape to the World monument's Fund 2006 watch list, these leading preservation organizations are working together to develop a strategic plan to address the threats that endanger this landscape and propose solutions to stem more extensive impact...Today's announcement serves as a reinforcement of our mission to preserve and protect it.[111]

Timothy DeWitt, of the Bluegrass Conservancy, asked:

> *How can we, the Greater Bluegrass Community, marshal our resources to best preserve this unique region? There are really only two ways to go—be passive and let events of the day prevail, or be proactive by defining in broader terms what makes this region so unique, and strategically set into place a shared vision and implement a holistic public policy that ensures sustainability of this region over time.*[112]

Many groups, both government sponsored and nonprofit, joined together in the fight to save the Bluegrass. While most of them were founded before inclusion on the watch list, the designation galvanized their efforts and shone a spotlight on their struggle. Each group is unique, as they serve different niches within the issue, but they work together to provide a solid voice against the misuse or destruction of farmland, historic structures and irresponsible growth, while promoting smart growth concepts in land-use planning.

## THE BLUEGRASS CONSERVANCY

The Bluegrass Conservancy works as a private, not-for-profit land trust throughout the Inner Bluegrass Region. The conservancy was founded in 1995 by concerned horseman and conservationists worried about the spread of sprawl and the lack of coordination among the counties in the region to contain it. Former Kentucky governor Brereton Jones and his wife, Libby, owners of Airdrie Farm, were instrumental in the formation of the group.

The mission of the group is to "encourage the preservation of these lands through the use of conservation easements for agricultural viability, natural habitat, rural heritage, and scenic open space."[113] All farms are eligible for protection; currently, easements are in place for cattle, tobacco and horses farms.

The process is tailored to meet the needs of each individual farm. The conservancy stresses that flexibility is important in the process because different farm owners have different needs and situations. Unlike the PDR programs, this is a land donation, which in most cases leads to significant reductions in federal income and estate taxes. One of the first farms to donate to the conservancy was a cattle farm in northern Jessamine County, owned by Bob and Ann Wilson. When asked about why they decided to donate the property rights, they replied that they "believed very strongly that

Airdrie Farm is permanently protected by conservation easement. *Photo by author.*

productive farmland is a trust for future generations," and the farm, which had been in the family since the 1920s, "should be preserved as an asset and not 'used up' like a commodity."[114]

Several prominent thoroughbred farms have donated to the Bluegrass Conservancy, including the 349-acre Middlebrook Farm, owned by Helen Thomas, home to several graded stakes winners and Eclipse Award winner Queena. The farm was an important piece of property, joining properties already, or planning to be, under easement protection, creating large tracts of preserved farmland.

Historically speaking, one of the most significant donations to the Bluegrass Conservancy would be the acquisition of Airdrie Stud, put under perpetual conservation by Brereton and Libby Jones. In 1972, this pristine property, containing structures dating to the eighteenth century, long stretches of dry stone walls and a pioneer cemetery, nearly became a 125-home subdivision called Charter Oaks. The former owner of the property proposed to re-zone the farmland, paving the way to development, only to see fierce opposition from local landowners and farmers.

Libby Jones recalls a group of twenty-five to thirty-five neighbors meeting at their home to not only protest but also form a plan to appeal to the Woodford County Planning and Zoning Commission. With over one hundred people protesting the development at the first public hearing, the commission voted unanimously to deny the zoning request, saving the farm and probably many of the neighboring farms, which would have instantly become prime development candidates.

One of these neighboring farms was the former R.A. Alexander's Woodburn Farm. In January 2003, the Joneses purchased the Woodburn property from a family member, primarily motivated to put the property under a conservation easement with the Bluegrass Conservancy.

## Fayette Alliance

The Fayette Alliance, based in Lexington, is an education and lobbying nonprofit organization dedicated to countywide land advocacy for Fayette County. Founded in 2006, the group is an ever-present voice at all relevant government meetings. The group was founded by concerned people within the horse industry to be a voice in the development of farmland. Over time, this voice expanded into the interrelated web of other land-based planning issues—everything from lobbying the local government for a bike trail taskforce and supporting Fayette County's PDR program to educating the public about the need for fixing city sewers.

The Fayette Alliance Board originally consisted of an impressive array of members of the Fayette County thoroughbred industry, including Greg Goodman, owner of Mount Brilliant Farm. Mount Brilliant was part of famed breeder and owner James Ben Ali Haggin's Elmendorf Farm for eighty-five years. Another parcel of the farm was owned by Colonel Barak Thomas, owner of the great nineteenth-century thoroughbred Domino, which is buried on the farm. Goodman also purchased an adjoining property, Faraway Farm, where Man o' War stood stud until his death in 1947. Although Goodman caught heat from the community for demolishing the circa 1792 mansion on the property, he worked with the University of Kentucky Department of Historic Preservation to restore Man o' War's dilapidated barn to its original condition.

Also on the original Fayette Alliance Board were farm owners Don Robinson of Winter Quarter Farm, breeder of the great race mare Zenyatta; Helen Alexander, owner of Middlebrook Farm; and John Phillips, managing partner at Darby Dan Farm, on the original property of E.R. Bradley's historic Idle Hour Stock Farm. Also represented were Keeneland's Nick Nicholson, Kentucky Horse Park director John Nicholson and Fasig-Tipton's Walt Robertson. Clearly, it was an organization composed of some of the most powerful and influential voices in the Fayette County community.

Chairman of the Fayette Alliance Board John Phillips likened the region to an industrial setting to make his point, saying, "In order for it to operate efficiently, we need to maintain the critical mass. Suburban sprawl intrudes upon our factory floor and there's incremental erosion to that floor."[115] The alliance stressed that it was not anti-growth but that preserving the rural exterior also meant promoting growth within downtown Lexington and within the Urban Services Boundary.

## Bluegrass Tomorrow

Bluegrass Tomorrow, a nonprofit coalition that serves as a conduit between public, private and corporate citizens in an eighteen-county area—outside the borders of the traditional Inner Bluegrass but encompassing the Bluegrass Area Development District. Bluegrass Tomorrow, dating its founding to the early 1990s, promotes a high quality of livability for the region, highlighting "clear, unique community identity, bearable traffic, alternative transportation, respect for cultural and agricultural heritage, clean environment and financially, environmentally, and socially responsible growth."[116]

Bluegrass Tomorrow's role in the fight against irresponsible growth is distinctive in several ways. Maybe most importantly, it monitors the entire Bluegrass Region, not just one community, serving as an essential communications piece between various counties. Private sector leadership is utilized, an important component when working across county lines. Furthermore, Bluegrass Tomorrow's leadership is composed of a variety of individuals from many different professional fields, strengthening the group's reach and impact. Accountants, farmers, educators, attorneys, developers, engineers and many more fields are represented in the group. While the focus of Bluegrass Tomorrow is for a high level of livability, the group asserts that it is "not beholden to any special interest groups."[117]

In an essay from 2002 for the *Lexington Herald Leader*, then-director Steve Austin writes of the need for cooperation and the need for a regional, rather than provincial, outlook when dealing with issues facing the region. He proposed what many viewed as a radical idea of ensuring that all the counties within the region had a high level of services, which meant sharing the need for a regional transportation organization, a regional planning commission and a regional environmental council. Of course, with implementation, these regional organizations would challenge or even supplant the provincial county leaderships, scaring some who saw it as "Lexington telling them what to do" and "local folks losing control of local decisions."[118]

## THE KENTUCKY THOROUGHBRED ASSOCIATION

The Kentucky Thoroughbred Association (KTA) is an organization that seeks to bring the many different parts of the thoroughbred industry together to provide a voice in issues affecting the industry. The KTA is involved in a variety of issues, from developing and administering a purse supplement fund and playing an active role in legislative matters affecting the industry to funding equine drug research. The KTA was also instrumental in developing Fayette County's PDR program and plays an active part in the Bluegrass Region as zoning and land-use issues arise.

Education and public information are other areas in which the KTA participates. An education outreach program run by the Kentucky Derby Museum based in Louisville is co-funded by the KTA. The outreach program visits tens of thousands of Kentucky schoolchildren every year, teaching the heritage and importance of the industry to the commonwealth. One of the programs offered is a social studies–based program for grades four through eight, called "Vanishing Bluegrass," concerning land-use issues.

"Vanishing Bluegrass" outreach programming, conducted by the Kentucky Derby Museum and cosponsored by the Kentucky Thoroughbred Association. *Photo by author.*

The KTA works statewide to promote the industry and puts things very succinctly: "No horse—no product—no owners—no income—no jobs. If we do nothing to protect our most important assets, horses and owners, our unique ability to breed and race will represent nothing but a memory."[119]

## THE KENTUCKY HERITAGE COUNCIL

Although preserving farmland related to the thoroughbred industry has been the primary focus, of course there are many other aspects of farmland property that are worthy of consideration. The wildlife, fauna, watershed and structures on the property are all extremely important as well and are certainly just as important to preserve. Whether it is rock walls that are common in the area, magnificent mansions representing many different architectural styles or the ornate barns that have housed champions from years past to today, the structures on these properties are a focus of the Kentucky Heritage Council.

The Kentucky Heritage Council, the state historic preservation office, encourages historic preservation as an important part of comprehensive planning and economic development. The council administers a tax credit program as an incentive for private investment in historic buildings.

Directly relating to suburban sprawl is the decline of most, if not all, downtown districts in the Bluegrass Region. The Kentucky Heritage Council developed the Kentucky Main Street Program to assist communities with revitalization efforts of the sagging downtown districts. The Inner Bluegrass Region towns of Danville, Georgetown, Harrodsburg, Lawrenceburg, Lexington, Midway, Nicholasville, Paris, Richmond, Shelbyville, Wilmore and Winchester all currently participate in the program. The council provides guidance and support for the participating towns.

Several of these towns have made great strides in downtown revitalization, thanks in large part to the support of the heritage council. Versailles has been recognized as a national Main Street Community, designated by the National Trust for Historic Preservation. The previous "deteriorating and increasingly deserted"[120] downtown of Versailles is now a thriving downtown district. The small college town of Midway has also enjoyed a renaissance, due in large part to investing in its downtown.

# The University of Kentucky College of Design

The University of Kentucky College of Design runs the university's Department of Historic Preservation. This graduate program offers students experience in study, research and local community activism. The department works with many other organizations in the fight against unchecked growth and preserving existing structures within the cultural landscape.

The College of Design researched and constructed the "Vanishing Bluegrass" exhibit for the Kentucky Derby Museum, which was produced in response to the region being named on the World Monument's Fund watch list in 2006.

# The Bluegrass Trust for Historic Preservation

The Bluegrass Trust for Historic Preservation, based in Lexington, is a nonprofit advocating historic preservation. The group is very involved in education programming, hosting lectures, Girl Scout retreats and exhibits. It is one of earliest preservation programs in the region, founded in 1955.

The most visible aspect of the group's presence is its plaque program, "serving as a visual symbol of civic pride and meant to signify respect and appreciation for the historic value of the properties."[121] The group's success is impressive. Structures that have been saved include Henry Clay's Law Office, the Mary Todd Lincoln House and Benjamin Latrobe's Pope Villa.

# Kentucky Equine Education Project (KEEP)

KEEP's mission is to increase awareness of the benefits of Kentucky's horse economy to promote jobs and economic opportunities. The group participates and is involved with a variety of issues that affect the industry—land use, legislation concerning expanded gaming and tax incentives for farm owners. The group is currently developing a grassroots, Kentucky-wide coalition whose goal is to educate the public and key state constituencies about the benefits of a strong equine economy.

Equine education is KEEP's focus, and the group provides several scholarships for students wishing to enter the equine industry. The group has given thousands of dollars in scholarships since the program began in 2007.

## THE EQUINE LAND CONSERVATION RESOURCE

The Equine Land Conservation Resource is a national organization based in Lexington. This group also exists as an education resource, as well as a vocal proponent for responsible land use. Unlike the groups listed above, this nonprofit organization includes in its scope all land used for horse-related activity and is geared toward "horse people." Preserving pastureland and trails is a focus of the group. The group encourages and instructs horse owners how to get involved in the issues and offers advice on how to maintain environmentally friendly actions.

It's true that many farms have been lost to unchecked growth, but there are successes as well. Success never gets as much publicity as when a property is developed, but it is important to note. Conservation and preservation are due to both the groups listed above and, of course, individual initiative.

The region's oldest continuously run thoroughbred farm is the Clay family's Runnymede Farm. The 365-acre Bourbon County farm was founded by Colonel Ezekiel Clay in 1867 and is under no consideration for development. Another Bourbon County institution is the venerated Claiborne Farm. Owned by the fourth generation of the Hancock family, the farm is under no pressure of development. Robert N. Clay's Three Chimneys Stud in Woodford County is a founding member of both the Bluegrass Conservancy and Bluegrass Tomorrow. Much of his 2,300-acre farm is under conservation easement.

The farm most associated with Kentucky's dominance over the thoroughbred industry throughout the twentieth century is Calumet Farm. Calumet bred and owned an astounding nine Kentucky Derby winners and is the only farm to have bred and owned two winners of thoroughbred racing's elusive Triple Crown: Whirlaway (1941) and Citation (1948).

The farm was founded by William Monroe Wright, owner of the Calumet Baking Powder Company, in 1924. Wright bred successful standardbreds on the farm, the best being Calumet Butler, winner of the prestigious Hambletonian in 1931. After Wright's death that same year, his son Warren took over the management of the farm, switching to the more lucrative thoroughbred breed soon after.

Success soon followed, with the purchase of filly Nelly Flag, which would run second in the Kentucky Derby and go on to become Calumet's first thoroughbred champion. But in 1936, Wright made two purchases that would secure Calumet's dominance for years to come and put Calumet in a class by itself, even among the established farms of the Bluegrass.

The first purchase was as part of a syndicate with Claiborne Farm, Greentree Farm and Stoner Creek Stud, buying the English sire Blenheim II. The stallion would produce many great runners, with his best being 1941 Triple Crown winner Whirlaway.

The other purchase was the eventual foundation sire of Calumet, Bull Lea. A son of Bull Dog, Wright bought Bull Lea for $14,000 from E. Dale Schaffer's Coldstream Stud (formerly McGrathiana). After a good racing career, winning ten times in twenty-seven starts, Bull Lea retired and went to stand stud at Calumet with good, but not great, expectations. He proved to be phenomenal. He was America's leading sire five times, producing fifty-eight stakes winners and nine champions. His progeny includes Twilight Tear, Armed, Coal Town, Two Lea and Bewitch. His greatest son was 1948 Triple Crown winner and first thoroughbred millionaire Citation, which many believe to be the greatest American racehorse ever. He also sired two other Derby winners: Hill Gail (1954) and Iron Liege (1957).

Warren Wright passed away in 1950, but his wife, Lucille Parker Wright (later Markey, after her marriage to Admiral Gene Markey in 1952), continued to breed top-quality thoroughbreds. The year 1964 would prove to be a pivotal one for the farm. Bull Lea died at the age of twenty-nine, and Jimmy Jones, longtime Calumet trainer (along with his father) retired. The farm continued to do well but did not dominate as it had decades before.

Admiral and Mrs. Markey both died in the early 1980s, leaving the farm to their daughter, Lucille "Cindy" Wright, and her husband, J.T. Lundy, who served as head of operations of the farm. Things seemed to pick up for Calumet, which won the 1990 Eclipse Award for Outstanding Breeder. But a year that began so well ended in suspicion, and eventually shock, as prized stallion Alydar died of a broken leg under mysterious circumstances. Calumet, struggling financially, had taken out a $36 million insurance policy on the stallion, making the accident heavily scrutinized. After an investigation that lasted a year, Lundy and one other Calumet employee were found guilty and sentenced to prison. The once-proud icon of Kentucky thoroughbred breeding, with its 762 pristine acres and barns trimmed in the devil's red, declared bankruptcy in 1991.

Many speculated that Calumet would be developed, as the price of land exploded in the housing boom of the early 1990s. The farm also sat within the Urban Services Boundary, making it not out of the question that the land would be developed. In 1992, Calumet went to the auction block, and the Bluegrass community looked on in apprehension.

First, household items and pieces of the farm's history were let go. The *New York Times* described, "$150 for a pair of stirrups, $9,000 for a silver cup, $23,000 for a painting of Alydar, $72,000 for the fully restored 1939 horse van, $5,000 for a 1978 tractor and $5,300 for a cast iron jockey in the devil's red silks."[122]

A two-hundred-foot-long tent was set up on the Calumet lawn, and the bidding for the farm itself began among three potential buyers: Henryk deKwiatkowski, Graham Beck of Lexington's Gainesway Farm and an unidentified bidder. The bidding started at $10 million, and ten minutes later, the farm sold for $17 million. The new owner was deKwiatkowski, a Polish-born businessman who made a fortune leasing and brokering the sale of used airplanes. There were probably many in the crowd of four thousand that day who were disappointed in the sale, unsure of deKwiatkowski's plans for the farm. Instead, he told the relieved crowd that he would "keep Calumet Farm alive…not a speck of grass will be changed."[123]

The farm may have been saved from possible development because of one man's determination to save it. But deKwiatkowski passed away in 2003, leaving the farm to heirs. Many wondered anew if the valuable property would once

Calumet Farm, quiet but intact. *Photo by author.*

"Coming Soon." *Photo by author.*

again go up for sale. The heirs quickly dispelled the rumors; there were no plans to sell. But years later, questions remain about the property. Currently, there are no stallions advertised as standing on the property. The website reveals a bare-bones staff. Under the "news" link, there is "no news at this time." The property looks the same from outside the gates, but no tours are given. Calumet is quiet.

This makes people in the Bluegrass nervous, as Calumet symbolizes what the Bluegrass Region is all about. Although the farm has not bred any champions for several years, it is still looked at as the pinnacle in breeding excellence, sitting majestically next door to Keeneland Race Course. If Calumet Farm can be developed, then nothing is sacred—any farm can be developed. Perhaps deKwiatkowski said it best when he told an interviewer in the days just after he bought the farm, "Wherever I turn, ordinary people, they call congratulations to me and say 'You saved our farm.' 'Our farm.'"[124] Perhaps that is what is so discomforting when a farm is developed—there are the economic issues, the environmental issues and the social issues, but more importantly, something unique about Kentucky is destroyed and turned into "Anyplace, USA." We lose an important part of who we are.

# Epilogue

Anyone interested in the important fight against suburban sprawl and in preserving an important piece of Kentucky's Bluegrass horse farms should please contact, learn about and support the following organizations:

Bluegrass Conservancy
380 South Mill Street, Suite 205
Lexington, KY 40508
(859) 255-4552
www.bluegrassconservancy.org

Bluegrass Tomorrow
P.O. Box 34185
Lexington, KY 40588
(859) 277-9614
www.bluegrasstomorrow.org

Bluegrass Trust for Historic Preservation
253 Market Street
Lexington, KY 40507
(859) 253-0362
www.bluegrasstrust.org

Equine Land Conservation Resource
4037 Iron Works Parkway, Suite 120
Lexington, KY 40511
(859) 455-8383
http://www.elcr.org/index.php

Fayette Alliance
603 Short Street
Lexington, KY 40508
(859) 281-1202
www.fayettealliance.org

Kentucky Equine Education Project
4037 Iron Works Parkway, Suite 130
Lexington, KY 40511
(859) 259-0007
www.horsework.com

Kentucky Heritage Council
300 Washington Street
Frankfort, KY 40601
(859) 564-7005
http://heritage.ky.gov

Kentucky Thoroughbred Association
4079 Iron Works Parkway
Lexington, KY 40511
(859) 381-1414
www.kta-ktob.com

University of Kentucky College of Design
117 Pence Hall
Lexington, KY 40506
(859) 257-7623
www.uky.edu/design

# NOTES

## CHAPTER 1

1. John D. Wright, *Lexington: Heart of the Bluegrass* (Lexington: University of Kentucky, 1994), 2.
2. Karl B. Raitz, "Bluegrass Culture," Pathways in Geography Series, University of Indiana, 1994, 23.
3. Thomas Jefferson, *Thomas Jefferson Farm Book*, commentary by Edwin Morris Betts (N.p.: University of North Carolina Press, 2002), 88.
4. "Henry Clay and Horse Racing," www.henryclay.org/henry-clay/farmer/henry-clay-and-horse-racing.
5. *Lexington Herald Leader*, May 17, 1903.

## CHAPTER 2

6. Otto Rothert, *A History of Muhlenberg County* (Louisville: John P. Morton and Co., 1913), Internet archive, www.archive.org/stream/historyofmuhlenb00roth/historyofmuhlenb00roth_djvu.txt.
7. Ibid.
8. Lexington History Museum, "Archives: Bluegrass Historian," www.lexingtonhistorymuseum.org/archives/historian/BGH/index.php.
9. John Dimon, *A Complete History of Horses and Horse Breeding* (Hartford, CT: John Dimon, 1895), 49.

10. Wikipedia, s.v., "Beriah Magoffin," http://en.wikipedia.org/wiki/Beriah_Magoffin#cite_ref-powell52_2-2.
11. Letter to Mary Belle Alexander Deedes, May 13, 1861; William Preston Mangum, *A Kingdom for the Horse* (Prospect, KY: Harmony House Publishers, 1999), 45.
12. Mangum, *Kingdom for the Horse*, 51.
13. Ibid., 57.
14. Ibid., 58.
15. "U.S Grant and his horses during and after the Civil War," http://faculty.css.edu/mkelsey/usgrant/hors1.html.
16. Mangum, *Kingdom for the Horse*, 99.
17. Robert Wickliffe Woolley, "Old Kentucky and the Thoroughbred," http://www.colbyfields.com/wp-content/uploads/2010/01/the-Old-Kentuckian.pdf.
18. *New York Times*, July 1875.

## CHAPTER 3

19. Samuel W. Thomas, *Churchill Downs: A Documentary History of America's Most Legendary Racetrack* (Louisville: Kentucky Derby Museum, 1995), 34.
20. "Derby Day," *Louisville Commercial*, April 25, 1875.
21. "Pool Selling on the Louisville Races," *New York Times*, May 16, 1875.
22. "The Louisville Races," *New York Times*, May 14, 1876.
23. "Apollo Wins," *Courier Journal*, May 17, 1882.
24. "At the Track," *Courier Journal*, May 15, 1883.
25. Thomas, *Churchill Downs*, 78.
26. "Racing Prospects at Louisville," *Thoroughbred Record*, July 28, 1894.

## CHAPTER 4

27. *Richardson's Southern Guide: A Complete Handbook to the Beauty Spots, Historical Places, Noted Battlefields, Famous Resorts, Principal Industries, and Chief Points of Interest of the South, "Chicago to Jacksonville"* (Chicago: Monarch Book Company, 1905), 32.
28. James Knowles, ed., *The Nineteenth Century*, vol. 27 (London: Kegan Paul, Trench and Co., 1890), 935.
29. *Louisville Times*, October 15, 1906.

30. "Famous Turf Plungers," *New York Times*, June 24, 1900.

31. Lynn Reneau, *Racing Around Kentucky* (Louisville: self-published, 1995).

32. James Duane Bolin, *Bossism and Reform in a Southern City: Lexington, Kentucky 1880–1940* (Lexington: University Press of Kentucky, 2000), 70.

33. Ibid.

34. Kenneth T. Jackson, *Crabgrass Frontier: The Suburbanization of the United States* (New York: Oxford University Press, 1985), 4.

35. Oliver Gillham and Alex S. McLean, *The Limitless City: A Primer on the Urban Sprawl Debate* (Washington, D.C.: The Island Press, 2002), 75.

## Chapter 5

36. William F. Reed, "When a Rabbit Won the Roses," *Sports Illustrated*, June 9, 1969.

37. Ibid.

38. "The Saratoga Races," *New York Times*, July 25, 1873.

39. Ibid.

40. "Big Red's Stable: The United Fans of Man o' War," www.network54.com/forum/21441.

41. "Sports of the Times," *New York Times*, August 28, 1932.

42. Ibid.

43. Obituary, *New York Times*, July 6, 1881.

44. "The Status of the American Turf," *Outing* 19 (1892): 478.

45. "McGrathiana Stud to Go," *New York Times*, July 6, 1908.

46. Ibid.

47. Interview with Dr. Joseph Wyse, www.thinkbluegrass.com.

48. Minutes of University of Kentucky Board of Trustees, December 13, 1989.

49. Ibid.

50. Susan Beniak, "New Designs on Coldstream," *Business Lexington*, October 16, 2008.

## Chapter 6

51. http://hamburgplace-lexington-ky.com/aboutus.aspx.

52. Kent Hollingsworth, *The Wizard of the Turf: John E. Madden of Hamburg Place* (N.p.: Bloodhorse, 1965), 13.

53. Ibid.

54. Edward Madden, *The Trotters at Hamburg Place, Lexington, KY, USA* (Cleveland, OH: Judson Printing Co., 1911), 127.

55. Ibid., 130.

56. Ibid.

57. Bruce McNall and Michael D'Antonio, *Fun While It Lasted: My Rise and Fall in the land of Fame and Fortune* (New York: Hyperion, 2003), 58.

58. Hollingsworth, *Wizard of the Turf.*

59. "Focus: Lexington; Intruders in Famed Bluegrass," *New York Times*, May 22, 1988.

60. "Interview with Anita Madden," *Lane Report*, July 2000.

61. "A Prince and his Place," *Lexington Herald Leader*, April 4, 2004.

62. Ibid.

63. "Interview with Patrick Madden," *Lane Report*, June 2007.

64. Letter from John E. Madden to H.M. Hanna, January 2, 1910, included in Madden, *Trotters at Hamburg Place*, 123.

65. "Decades Old Horse Graves Moved for Shopping Center," *USA Today*, July 26, 2005.

66. "One Likens Flowers to Make-up on a Corpse," *Lexington Herald Leader*, May 11, 2005.

67. Fall 2000 Sprawl Report, www.sierraclub.org/sprawl/50statesurvey/Kentucky.asp.

68. "Planners Are Deciding Where to Draw the Lines," *Lexington Herald Leader*, April 17, 2006.

69. Ibid.

70. "Interview with Anita Madden."

71. "Interview with Patrick Madden."

## CHAPTER 7

72. Unknown newspaper clipping dated May 12, 1892, from Bashford Manor scrapbook, Kentucky Derby Museum collections.

73. Bert McKenna, *Who's Who in Horsedom*, vol. IV (Lexington, KY: Ransom Publishing Co., 1951), 115.

74. John E. Kleber, *The Encyclopedia of Louisville* (Lexington: University Press of Kentucky, 2001), 229.

75. Thoroughbred Heritage website, www.tbheritage.com/portraits/alarm.html.

76. Ibid.

77. "Falsetto, Old Turf King, Dying," *New York Times*, July 23, 1904.
78. *Louisville Evening Post*, May 12, 1892.
79. Unknown source, clipping found in Bashford Manor scrapbook, Kentucky Derby Museum.
80. Ibid.
81. Ibid.
82. "Long Shots Win at Gravesend Track," *New York Times*, May 30, 1900.
83. *Courier Journal*, May 3, 1906.
84. Ibid.
85. Clipping in Bashford Manor scrapbook.
86. *Daily Racing Form*, October 22, 1918.
87. Unknown newspaper clipping dated May 7, 1970, from Bashford Manor scrapbook, Kentucky Derby Museum collections.
88. *Courier Journal*, January 13, 1911.
89. Ibid., September 18, 2003.

## Chapter 8

90. Arthur C. Nelson, "Effects of Urban Containment on Housing Prices and Homeowner Behavior," Lincoln Institute of Land Policy, May 2000.
91. Ibid.
92. "Bluegrass Put on Watch List," *Lexington Herald Leader*, June 22, 2005.
93. "Is More Development Needed?" *Lexington Herald Leader*, April 4, 2004.
94. "Planners are Deciding Where to Draw the Lines," *Lexington Herald Leader*, http://www.skyscrapercity.com/showthread.php?t=181507&page=1.
95. Ibid.
96. Ibid.
97. Ibid.
98. "Lexington Planning Commission Takes Steps to Prevent Urban Sprawl," *Bloodhorse*, January 23, 2007.
99. "Land Survey Helps Guide Planning Process and Ideologies will Clash as Debate Heats Up," *Lexington Herald Leader*, http://www.skyscrapercity.com/showthread.php?t=181507&page=15.
100. "Purchase of Development Rights," Lexington Fayette Urban County Government, 2010 Planning Commission Update, PowerPoint.
101. "Land-Preservation Program Experiences Growing Pains," *Bloodhorse*, June 3, 2002.
102. "Padua Buys Bluegrass Heights Farm," *Bloodhorse*, March 13, 2008.

103. Woodford County Planning and Zoning Commission, http://planning.woodfordcountyky.org/documents/RC%20Prologue%20and%20Chapter%201.pdf.

104. "Property Rights, Preservation Clash in Central Kentucky," *Bloodhorse*, April 17, 2007.

105. Ibid.

106. Ibid.

107. Ibid.

108. World Monuments Fund website, http://www.wmf.org/sites/default/files/wmf_article/pg_14-19_bluegrass.pdf.

109. Kentucky Derby Museum archives, "Vanishing Bluegrass" files.

110. Ibid.

111. Ibid.

112. Ibid.

113. Bluegrassconservancy.org.

114. Ibid.

115. "Horse Industry Mobilizes to Protect Fayette Farmland," *Bloodhorse*, June 8, 2006.

116. www.bluegrasstomorrow.org.

117. Ibid.

118. Ibid.

119. http://www.kta-ktob.com/AboutUs/WhoWeAre.aspx.

120. Preserve America Community: Versailles, Kentucky, http://www.preserveamerica.gov/firstPAcommunities-versaillesKY.html.

121. http://bluegrasstrust.org/aboutus.html.

122. "Memories are Sold, Farm Stays," *New York Times*, March 29, 1992.

123. Ibid.

124. Ibid.

# ABOUT THE AUTHOR

Ronnie Dreistadt has worked for the Kentucky Derby Museum for thirteen years and is considered an expert on the history of the race. He has written several newspaper/magazine articles pertaining to general Kentucky Derby history and has been the outreach education coordinator for the Kentucky Derby Museum for eight years. He has also written and researched all of the tours the Kentucky Derby museum now offers: historic walking tour, barn and backside stable tour, behind the scenes tour and the horses and haunts tour (ghost stories). He has researched and written six education programs, including the "Vanishing Bluegrass" program, on which much of this book is based. This program was developed and produced for grades five through eight in 2007 and was adapted and expanded for an adult audience in 2010. Originally, this topic was the subject of a temporary exhibit displayed in the Kentucky Derby Museum.

Visit us at

www.historypress.net